À LA DÉCOUVERTE DE L'AMÉRIQUE

Marc Cantin et Isabel
Illustrations intérieures : Nils

Une série conçue par Philippe Alessandri

Nathan

Le professeur Théodore Champollion a disparu! Mina est convaincue qu'il est arrivé quelque chose à son grand-père. Avec ses deux meilleurs amis, Mathis et Robin, elle mène l'enquête dans le musée du savant. Dans une pièce secrète, ils découvrent… une machine à remonter le temps! Construite par Théodore, elle lui servait à explorer le passé pour y scanner des objets et exposer leur reproduction virtuelle dans son musée. Appelée Rose, la machine explique aux trois amis que le professeur est resté bloqué dans les couloirs du temps.

Pour le délivrer, une seule solution : les enfants doivent mener à bien chacun des voyages qu'il avait programmés et numériser pour le musée l'objet qu'avait prévu de rapporter le professeur. Mais attention, ils ne doivent pas rester plus de deux heures dans chaque époque.

Le compte à rebours est enclenché : 5, 4, 3, 2, 1… Embarque avec Mina, Mathis et Robin pour une nouvelle aventure dans le passé !

Mina, 12 ans

Mina adore son grand-père.
Il faut dire qu'ils partagent
la même passion pour l'Histoire. Alors,
quand il disparaît, elle n'a qu'une idée
en tête : le retrouver. Même si cela signifie
affronter mille dangers. Heureusement
qu'elle sait garder la tête froide…

Mathis, 12 ans

L'aventure, Mathis en rêve.
Le sportif de la bande n'a peur
de rien ! Et ce n'est pas une nouvelle mission
de Rose qui va l'effrayer. Plutôt foncer !
Quitte à provoquer des catastrophes… mais
que ne ferait-il pas pour impressionner Mina !

Robin, 12 ans

Le garçon préfère la diplomatie
à la force, le calme au danger.
S'il a parfois du mal à suivre ses deux amis,
jamais il ne les laisserait partir sans lui.

Voyager dans le temps, au fond, c'est passionnant… et pas question de laisser Mathis faire son intéressant avec Mina!

Rose
La machine à remonter le temps aide les enfants dans leurs missions. Grâce à elle, ils parlent la langue de la civilisation visitée et sont en tenue d'époque. Elle leur fournit aussi des informations utiles. Mais attention, elle a son petit caractère!

Le GTS (Guide Temporel du Système)
Ce bracelet permet aux enfants de communiquer avec Rose et de se repérer pendant leurs missions. Il fonctionne comme un GPS, indiquant où nos trois héros se trouvent et le point R (le point de retour) où ils doivent se rendre. Il leur donne aussi des informations sur l'époque visitée.

* Tu trouveras les mots suivis d'une étoile expliqués par Rose à la fin du livre.

1
Un look étrange

Assis sur un banc, Mina et Robin attendent Mathis en face de l'école de musique. Leur copain y suit des cours, chaque mercredi, depuis que ses parents ont décrété qu'il devait apprendre à jouer d'un instrument.

– Comment peuvent-ils avoir de telles idées ? s'interroge Mina en regardant sa montre. Ils savent pourtant que Mathis préfère le sport.

Robin esquisse un sourire :

– Quand il a su que la première année était consacrée au solfège, il a bien failli s'évanouir ! Ha ! Ha !

– Arrête de rire, le prévient Mina. Le voilà qui arrive.

— Il a l'air encore de mauvaise humeur, chuchote Robin.

Les mains dans les poches et la tête rentrée dans les épaules, Mathis affiche un regard orageux. À l'inverse, l'élève qui l'accompagne semble radieux, même si son look n'a rien de joyeux : il est habillé tout en noir, ses cheveux bruns lui cachent la moitié du visage et ses doigts sont couverts de bagues en forme de tête de mort !

Mathis s'arrête devant Mina et Robin et désigne son camarade d'un coup de menton.

— Je vous présente Dark, grommelle-t-il.

— Nous devons rendre un travail en commun la semaine prochaine, explique le garçon au look étrange. Trop cool, non ?

Il échange sa clé MP3 avec celle de Mathis et salue les trois amis.

— Je vais chercher ma petite sœur à la garderie, s'excuse-t-il.

Il leur adresse un signe de la main avant de s'éloigner.

— Les enfants vont hurler en le voyant, pouffe Mina.

— C'est peut-être de l'humour... noir ! ajoute Robin.

— Riez, mais moi je dois présenter un exposé sur une chanson avec ce gars. Vous imaginez comme ça va être drôle de travailler avec lui ! Et je ne vous parle pas de ses goûts musicaux.

— Je ne préfère pas, grimace Robin.

— C'est pour choisir votre chanson que vous avez échangé vos clés ? devine Mina.

Mathis hoche la tête.

Il branche son casque sur le MP3 et s'apprête à l'allumer.

– Tu écouteras ça plus tard, l'interrompt Mina. Rose nous attend.

– Allez, on y va ! s'impatiente Robin.

Mathis glisse la clé dans sa poche et part avec ses amis rejoindre le musée de Théodore Champollion, le grand-père de Mina.

2
Un départ désorganisé

Après avoir traversé le parc de la ville, Mina, Robin et Mathis entrent dans le prestigieux Musée virtuel du professeur Champollion. Ils empruntent la porte de service et accèdent en toute discrétion au bureau de l'archéologue. Ce dernier, toujours prisonnier des couloirs du temps, a laissé à sa petite-fille un pendentif qui permet d'ouvrir son laboratoire. À l'aide du bijou en forme de rose des vents, Mina débloque une porte dérobée et pénètre la première dans la salle secrète. Les enfants y retrouvent Rose, la machine à remonter le temps inventée par Théodore.

— **Bonjour**, les salue celle-ci. **Je commençais à m'ennuyer et j'avais hâte de vous revoir.**

— C'est vrai que vous n'avez pas beaucoup d'amis ! plaisante Robin.

L'imposante machine, dont le squelette est constitué de composants électroniques recouvrant les quatre murs de la pièce, n'apprécie pas la moquerie. Derrière ses parois transparentes, ses voyants, diodes et tubes virent au rouge.

— Mais je suis sûre que vous avez profité de ce temps pour préparer notre nouvelle mission, tempère Mina. Auriez-vous la gentillesse de nous dévoiler notre destination ?

Rose reprend des couleurs moins vives et décrit d'une voix appliquée l'épreuve qui attend le trio.

— **Vous devrez scanner l'anneau* en or offert par la tribu des Taïnos à Christophe Colomb lors de sa découverte de l'Amérique.**

Les trois amis échangent un regard.

— **Comme toujours,** ajoute Rose, **vous aurez deux heures pour accomplir cette mission.**

— Qui portera le GTS ? l'interroge Mathis.

Un silence envahit la pièce. Une trappe pivote et le bracelet électronique apparaît, accroché à l'extrémité d'une tige télescopique.

– **Lancement du programme. Synchronisation du Guide Temporel du Système. Porteur : Robin.**

– Pfff ! Je m'en doutais, se plaint Mathis.

– La prochaine fois, il sera pour toi, lui murmure son copain en ajustant le GTS à son poignet.

Pendant ce temps, Rose poursuit :

– **Création d'une boucle temporelle de deux heures : OK. Génération du filtre holographique en cours... Ouverture de la porte : dix secondes. Époque : 1492. Lieu : navire de Christophe Colomb. Objet à numériser : anneau d'or.**

Les lumières s'éteignent progressivement.

– **7, 6...** décompte Rose.

– Zut ! s'exclame Mathis. Je ne peux pas partir avec le lecteur MP3 de Dark. Je risque de le perdre.

– **4, 3, 2...** continue la machine.

Pendant que Rose poursuit le décompte, Mathis le sort de sa poche et se dépêche de l'accrocher à la tige télescopique qui retenait le GTS.

– Je vous le confie, Rose, dit-il en pointant un doigt vers la machine.

– **Filtre temporel en place!** termine celle-ci d'une voix imperturbable.

Mina et Robin ont déjà sauté à l'intérieur du cercle holographique multicolore apparu sur le sol.

– Hééé! Attendez-moi! s'écrie Mathis.

Le cercle commence à diminuer, quand le jeune garçon bondit pour le traverser avant qu'il ne se referme!

3
Naufragés en vue

02 h 00

La première chose que Robin distingue en ouvrant les yeux, c'est une planche en bois.

« Où suis-je ? songe-t-il. Ah, oui. Rose nous a envoyés sur le navire de Christophe Colomb. Donc, je suis sur un bateau. »

Il se rassure un instant… le temps de relever la tête.

– Aaaah ! s'écrie-t-il. Cette machine est détraquée !

L'embarcation sur laquelle il se trouve ne ressemble en rien à un navire. Il vogue sur une chaloupe en partie brisée qui mériterait davantage le nom de radeau !

— Calme-toi.

Robin reconnaît la voix de Mina et se tourne vers son amie. Elle porte une ample chemise blanche en vieille toile et un pantalon élimé qui s'arrête à mi-mollet. Robin baisse la tête pour constater qu'il est habillé de la même façon.

— N... nous sommes en pleine mer ! bafouille-t-il. Rose s'est trompée !

— Je ne crois pas, tente de le rassurer Mina.

Elle invite Robin à se retourner. Ce dernier écarquille les yeux en découvrant trois bateaux qui se dirigent vers eux.

— Deux caravelles* et une nef*, reprend Mina. Christophe Colomb navigue sûrement sur le plus grand d'entre eux. Je pense que Rose nous a mis sur sa route afin qu'il nous prenne pour des naufragés.

— Alors, tout va bien ? se réjouit Robin.

— Pas vraiment, lui avoue son amie. Mathis n'est pas avec nous.

Robin se raidit et tourne inutilement la tête

dans tous les sens pour inspecter la barque où il se trouve.

– Tu crois qu'il est bloqué dans les couloirs du temps, comme ton grand-père ?

– Il semblait tellement préoccupé par son exposé qu'il a peut-être raté l'ouverture de la porte, suppose Mina. Dans ce cas, il est resté dans le présent et il ne craint rien. Nous, en revanche, nous devons nous concentrer sur notre mission et monter absolument sur le navire de Christophe Colomb.

La jeune aventurière se met debout pour adresser des signes aux bateaux. Robin se lève à son tour et agite les bras, autant pour attirer l'attention des navigateurs que pour essayer de conserver son équilibre sur l'embarcation qui épouse le mouvement des vagues.

– Au secours ! hurle Mina. Aidez-nous !

En haut du grand mât de la nef, la vigie pointe un doigt vers la chaloupe et crie :

– Naufragés à tribord ! Naufragés à tribord !

Le plus imposant des trois navires ajuste aussitôt son cap… mais il ne réduit pas sa vitesse en approchant de l'embarcation.

– I… ils vont nous faire chavirer ! panique Robin.

Des marins apparaissent le long du garde-corps de la nef, des cordages à la main.

– Ils ne comptent pas s'arrêter et il faudra s'agripper aux cordes qu'ils nous lanceront. Ça va secouer, prévient Mina.

Robin sent son cœur tambouriner comme s'il voulait sortir de sa poitrine pour s'enfuir loin d'ici. Le jeune garçon avale péniblement sa salive, se rassoit et s'accroche au bord de la chaloupe. Celle-ci risque de ne pas résister aux remous provoqués par la nef.

— Ça ira ? lui demande Mina.

— On n'a pas le choix.

— C'est vrai, admet son amie alors que l'imposant bateau n'est plus qu'à quelques mètres d'eux. Il n'y a pas de plan B.

4
Tensions à bord

01 h 49

Les remous provoqués par la nef agitent la chaloupe. Les premières vagues passent par-dessus bord et l'eau remplit à moitié la coque. Mina et Robin tendent les bras pour attraper les cordes lancées par les marins. Ils s'y agrippent de toutes leurs forces !

– Hissez les naufragés ! crie la vigie.

Les enfants s'envolent dans les airs, laissant derrière eux leur chaloupe qui commence à couler.

– Je vais mouriiir ! gémit Robin.

Suspendu au bout du cordage, le long de la paroi du navire, Robin est remonté vers le pont par les marins à la seule force de leurs bras. À côté de lui, plus à l'aise dans cet exercice, Mina prend appui avec ses pieds sur la coque de la nef.

– Tiens bon ! crie-t-elle à Robin. On sera bientôt en sécurité !

– En sécurité avec toi ? se plaint son ami. Ce serait bien la première fois !

Mina n'a pas le temps de répondre. Des mains la saisissent et la hissent à bord. L'instant d'après, elle atterrit sur le pont du navire en compagnie de Robin.

– On est sauvés ! se réjouit-elle

– T… Tu en es sûre ? doute son copain.

Des marins à la mine patibulaire entourent les deux rescapés. Certains sourient, laissant apparaître une dentition en pointillés, d'autres n'ont qu'un œil, celui qui manque étant caché par un bandeau, et tous portent de nombreuses cicatrices sur le visage. L'un d'entre eux arbore même fièrement une jambe de bois.

— Des pirates ! s'affole Robin.

— Hé ! Pas d'insulte, petit ! proteste un marin en sortant un couteau de sa poche.

— Nous dérivons depuis plusieurs jours, intervient aussitôt Mina, et le soleil a tapé sur la tête de mon ami.

— Il n'a peut-être pas tout son esprit, admet un barbu au visage balafré, mais il mérite quand même qu'on lui coupe un bout de langue pour oser nous offenser ainsi.

— Juan a raison, approuvent les autres. Un bout de langue, c'est juste.

— J… je m'excuse, assure Robin sans parvenir à quitter des yeux la lame du couteau.

— Que se passe-t-il ? demande alors une voix puissante.

Un homme élancé, vêtu d'un étroit pourpoint à taillades et d'un large manteau liseré de fourrure, se dirige vers eux.

— Je vous ai ordonné de récupérer les naufragés et non de les découper en morceaux, gronde-t-il. Tous à vos postes ! Immédiatement !

— Bien, amiral, grognent les marins.

Ils s'écartent et retournent à leur tâche, visiblement à contrecœur. Seul Juan, en qualité de maître d'équipage, reste auprès des deux enfants.

– Nous étions mousses à bord d'un navire français, explique immédiatement Mina. Mais une tempête a détruit notre bateau. Nous avons juste eu le temps de mettre une chaloupe à la mer.

– La chance est avec vous, mes amis, se réjouit l'amiral. Si vous pouviez m'en faire profiter un peu, j'en serais très heureux.

– Tout le plaisir serait pour nous, approuve Mina en s'inclinant.

– Voilà des naufragés très bien élevés, apprécie l'homme. Prends-en de la graine, Juan.

Le maître d'équipage hausse les épaules et jette un regard dédaigneux aux enfants.

– Je m'appelle Christophe Colomb, reprend l'amiral, et je suis en route pour les Indes*. Accompagnez-moi dans ma cabine, nous pourrons y discuter à notre aise.

Mina et Robin suivent le célèbre navigateur

qui leur ouvre la porte de la dunette. Ils accèdent ainsi au logement de l'officier. Ce dernier commande à Juan d'attendre sur le pont, ce qui accentue la mauvaise humeur du maître d'équipage.

– Les marins ont raison, grogne-t-il. L'amiral n'a plus toute sa tête.

5
En terre inconnue

01 h 44

Comme ses deux amis, Mathis est bien arrivé en 1492. Seulement, à la différence de Mina et Robin, il ne se trouve pas en mer… mais sur la terre ferme. Il s'étire, bâille plusieurs fois et se redresse lentement. Il laisse glisser entre ses doigts une poignée du magnifique sable fin sur lequel il s'est endormi. Puis il écarquille les yeux en découvrant qu'il est assis au milieu d'une plage tropicale !

– Ouah ! Le rêve ! chuchote-t-il pour lui-même. Rose a peut-être jugé que nous méritions des vacances.

Il remarque alors qu'il est vêtu d'un simple pagne, très court, qui s'avère agréable sous ce soleil éclatant.

— Robin ? Mina ? appelle-t-il.

Personne ne lui répond. Il se retourne et constate qu'il est seul. Malgré la chaleur, un léger frisson lui traverse le dos.

— Kriiiiiii !

Mathis sursaute en entendant ce cri au-dessus de sa tête. Il lève les yeux et aperçoit des oiseaux noirs de grande envergure.

— Des vautours ! s'exclame-t-il.

Les rapaces planent avec patience, décrivant des cercles autour de lui. Le jeune garçon agite les bras pour les chasser.

— Hé ! Je ne suis pas mort ! Allez chercher votre repas ailleurs !

Les oiseaux émettent de nouveaux cris et, déçus, reprennent de l'altitude. Mathis en profite pour s'éloigner. D'un pas rapide, il remonte la plage bordée de palmiers et de cocotiers. Au-delà, la forêt forme un rideau vert, mais, sur le haut d'une colline, il aperçoit les toits d'une dizaine de huttes.

« J'y retrouverai sûrement Mina et Robin », pense-t-il.

Une fumée s'élève du petit village. Il quitte la plage et se fraye un chemin dans la végétation. Bientôt, une agréable odeur de ragoût lui effleure les narines.

– Je parie que les autres ont réussi à se faire inviter à manger, se réjouit-il. J'ai hâte de connaître les spécialités locales !

Il accélère l'allure, saute par-dessus un arbre mort et découvre un sentier qui gravit la colline vers les huttes. Mais un craquement sous ses pieds retient son attention. Il s'arrête, baisse la tête… et ses yeux s'écarquillent comme des soucoupes.

– D… des os ! bafouille-t-il.

Ils s'étalent au milieu du passage, recouvrant presque le petit chemin. Un peu plus loin, celui-ci est bordé de piquets sur lesquels sont disposés des crânes !

« Je suis tombé au milieu d'une tribu de cannibales ! songe Mathis. Pourvu que Mina et Robin ne soient pas entre leurs mains ! »

6
Révolte à bord

01 h 37

Dans sa cabine richement meublée, Christophe Colomb désigne des fauteuils à Robin et Mina. Les enfants s'installent devant le bureau recouvert de cartes* marines.

— C'est un signe du destin qui m'a fait changer de cap pour vous secourir, leur confie le navigateur. Je suis sûr que vous allez me porter bonheur.

— Auriez-vous des ennuis ? demande Mina.

Christophe Colomb affiche un air soucieux. Il se penche vers les deux naufragés et leur confie à voix basse que ses marins sont à bout.

– Je leur avais promis de rejoindre les Indes en un mois, chuchote-t-il, mais voilà déjà plus de soixante jours que nous sommes en mer.

– Le double ! s'exclame Robin.

– Chut ! s'affole l'amiral. Mes hommes deviennent agressifs. Ils ont déjà menacé de me jeter par-dessus bord.

On frappe alors à la porte. Juan apparaît et, après avoir jeté un regard noir à Mina et Robin, il s'adresse à Christophe Colomb :

– Le vent se lève et l'équipage veut savoir quelle direction prendre.

– J'arrive, répond l'amiral d'une voix hésitante. Dis-leur d'attendre un peu.

– La patience n'est pas leur fort, rappelle le maître d'équipage. Et l'épuisement de nos réserves de vin n'arrange pas les choses !

Des bruits de fers qui s'entrechoquent ne laissent rien présager de bon. Colomb fronce les sourcils et se rend sur le pas de la porte pour tenter de calmer les marins. Mina se penche vers Robin.

– S'ils se mutinent, nous sommes cuits.

– Que faut-il faire ? murmure son ami.

– Interroge Rose pendant que Christophe Colomb et Juan sont occupés. Elle va nous aider à regagner la terre.

Robin acquiesce et, sous le bureau, il active le GTS.

– S'il vous plaît, Rose, quelle direction Colomb doit-il prendre pour découvrir l'Amérique au plus vite ?

> **C'est un grand navigateur. Il devrait très bien y arriver seul.**
> **Temps restant : 01 h 34 min 38 s.**

– Ce n'est pas sûr car nous l'avons dévié de sa route, rétorque Robin. Il y voit un signe du destin et il est persuadé que nous allons l'aider.

> **Les hommes me surprendront toujours. Contrairement à nous, les machines, vous êtes terriblement superstitieux*. Bien... dans ce cas, mettez le cap vers le nord-ouest. Bonne chance !**
> **Temps restant : 01 h 34 min 12 s.**

— Et Mathis ? demande Robin. Où est-il ?

> Euh... J'effectue justement des recherches à ce sujet en ce moment. Tout devrait rentrer dans l'ordre rapidement. Enfin, je l'espère.
> Temps restant : 01 h 34 min 01 s.

Le GTS s'éteint et les deux enfants échangent un regard angoissé.

— Nous devons continuer, dit enfin Mina d'une voix tremblante. Nous n'avons pas d'autre choix.

Elle attrape une boussole et une longue-vue sur le bureau de Colomb avant d'entraîner son ami à l'extérieur de la cabine. Sur le pont, les marins lèvent le poing en direction de l'amiral. Certains brandissent même leur épée ! Christophe Colomb hésite toujours sur les ordres à donner quand Mina, le nez sur la boussole, se dirige à tribord du navire. Arrivée près du garde-corps, elle observe l'horizon à la longue-vue de l'amiral.

— Des oiseaux ! s'écrie-t-elle. J'aperçois des oiseaux !

7
Terre en vue

01 h 32

La nouvelle apportée par Mina soulève la joie des marins et de Christophe Colomb.

— Ces oiseaux sont la preuve que la terre est proche, se réjouit le navigateur. Les naufragés nous portent chance !

— Quels sont vos ordres, amiral ? lui demande Juan.

— Réduisez la voilure pour gagner de l'allure. Le vent est avec nous et nous rejoindrons rapidement les côtes.

Colomb envoie Mina en haut des mâts pour exécuter la manœuvre avec les autres marins. Juan, dépité, la regarde grimper aux cordages avec ses hommes.

— Une fille sur les mâts, grogne-t-il, cela va nous porter malheur !

Mais l'amiral Colomb ignore ses remarques. Il a retrouvé tout son allant et son assurance.

— Parés pour la prise de ris ! annonce-t-il. Choquez l'écoute de grand-voile.

La voile est alors légèrement descendue au-dessous du point d'armure.

— Donnez encore un peu de mou à la drisse, continue Colomb. Étarquez la bosse de ris et réglez la tension de la voile pour qu'elle prenne bien le vent. Bravo, Mina ! Tu t'en sors très bien !

Le maître d'équipage est furieux. C'est lui qui devrait être à la place de cette fille avec les hommes ! Il profère quelques jurons qui finissent par déplaire à l'amiral.

— File sur le pont rejoindre l'équipe de nettoyage ! lui ordonne Christophe Colomb.

Juan s'éloigne en marmonnant des paroles inaudibles, mais le regard qu'il lance à Robin en le croisant est plus éloquent que n'importe quels mots!

– Terre! Terre! hurle Mina à tue-tête.

Robin lève les yeux et découvre son amie en haut du grand mât en compagnie de la vigie. Il savait que Mina avait du cran, mais aujourd'hui elle l'épate complètement. L'amiral pose une main sur l'épaule du jeune garçon.

– Tu vas m'aider à calculer le temps qu'il nous faut pour rejoindre la terre, déclare-t-il. Jette le loch à la mer.

Il confie à Robin un morceau de bois lesté en forme de triangle. Celui-ci, relié à la nef par une ligne enroulée sur une bobine, permet d'estimer la vitesse du bateau. Pendant que Robin s'exécute, Christophe Colomb utilise un sablier* pour mesurer le temps et un astrolabe pour déterminer sa position en mer.

– Nous toucherons terre dans moins de cinq sabliers ! déclare-t-il en pointant un doigt vers la côte qui se dessine à l'horizon.

C'est l'explosion de joie sur le pont. Colomb serre Robin dans ses bras et ordonne de préparer des chaloupes pour accoster.

8
Grosse frayeur

01 h 24

Après être resté beaucoup trop longtemps les yeux fixés sur les crânes exposés de chaque côté du chemin, Mathis pivote sur lui-même et décampe à grandes enjambées.

« Fuir ! Fuir ! » se répète-t-il en allongeant encore sa foulée.

La panique le gagne et il ne songe à rien d'autre que se mettre à l'abri du danger. Mais soudain, il aperçoit un groupe d'hommes au corps en partie recouvert de peinture noire, blanche et rouge. Ils sortent de la forêt et remontent le chemin droit vers lui.

« S'ils me voient, ils vont me manger ! » s'affole le pauvre Mathis.

Il fait à nouveau demi-tour et reprend la direction du village.

Il rejoint très vite l'endroit où sont entreposés les ossements et, à la vue de ces derniers, quitte le chemin. Il court se cacher derrière un rocher. Sitôt à l'abri, il s'assoit, le dos contre la pierre, ramène ses genoux à hauteur de son menton et tente de reprendre son souffle qui commence sérieusement à lui manquer.

– Tu as vu un mauvais esprit ? lui demande une voix.

Mathis sursaute et pose la main sur son cœur. Une jeune fille, juchée sur le haut du rocher, le dévisage.

– Tu es très peureux, juge-t-elle.

Elle doit avoir le même âge que Mathis et, comme les hommes, elle porte des peintures sur le corps. Des bijoux en or ornent également son cou et ses oreilles.

– D'où viens-tu ? demande-t-elle en sautant du rocher.

Elle atterrit devant Mathis, réduisant à néant tout espoir de fuite.

– Eh bien ? s'impatiente-t-elle. Quelqu'un a mangé ta langue ?

Les yeux du garçon s'arrondissent.

– T... tu vas me dévorer ? parvient-il à bredouiller. Comme ceux dont il ne reste que les os exposés là-bas ?

La jeune fille éclate de rire.

– Je m'appelle Yuma, et même si j'ai un peu faim, je ne te toucherai pas. Ces os sont ceux de nos ancêtres. Nous les plaçons à l'entrée du village pour que leur esprit veille sur nous et sur nos visiteurs.

– Alors personne ne les a mangés ?

– Je te le promets, sourit Yuma. Sois le bienvenu ici.

Les joues de Mathis s'enflamment. Il se sent ridicule d'avoir songé que cette jeune fille était une cannibale.

– Je suis désolé, s'excuse-t-il en se relevant. Je m'appelle Mathis et... je viens de loin. J'aime beaucoup voyager.

– Je suis heureuse de te connaître, Mathis,

dit Yuma en lui prenant la main. Je vais te présenter à ma famille et à mes amis.

Elle entraîne son invité avec elle. Mathis est ravi de cette rencontre et il espère de tout cœur retrouver Mina et Robin au village.

9
Des habitants pacifiques

01 h 11

À peine arrivé au village, Mathis est entouré par les habitants. Ceux-ci l'accueillent avec gentillesse et bienveillance, en particulier leur chef, Zumo. De taille moyenne, il se distingue des autres hommes par les nombreux colliers de perles et de coquillages qui pendent à son cou. Ils se chevauchent, formant une épaisse couche de bijoux qui tintent comme des clochettes à chacun de ses pas.

– Je suis le père de Yuma, explique Zumo. Et nous sommes la tribu des Taïnos.

Mathis, qui comprend parfaitement la

langue de Zumo grâce à Rose, sait que le nom de cette tribu signifie « nous sommes des hommes de bien ». Ce détail achève de le rassurer. Ses hôtes lui apportent alors du ragoût et des goyaves* qu'il s'empresse de goûter.

– Où se trouve ton village ? l'interroge soudain Yuma. Je ne t'ai jamais rencontré auparavant.

Un morceau de goyave reste coincé dans la gorge de Mathis. Que dire ? Que raconter ? Il doit absolument inventer une histoire plausible.

Pendant qu'il tousse pour faire passer le morceau de fruit, une idée lui traverse l'esprit. Il pointe un doigt vers l'océan que l'on peut admirer de la colline où est installé le village.

– Je vis sur une île et j'ai voulu explorer les environs avec ma barque. Hélas, une tempête s'est levée et m'a entraîné loin de chez moi. J'ai fini par échouer sur la plage.

– Oh ! Quel grand malheur ! compatit Zumo.

– J'avais aussi deux amis avec moi. Vous ne les avez pas vus ?

Les Taïnos présents hochent négativement la tête. Ils plaignent également le jeune garçon et promettent de l'aider à retrouver sa tribu et ses amis.

– Si nous n'y parvenons pas, ajoute Yuma, tu pourras toujours rester ici, avec nous.

Mathis est touché par cette proposition... et troublé par le ravissant sourire que lui adresse Yuma.

– Avant de partir à leur recherche, je vais peindre ton visage, lui propose-t-elle. Ainsi, tu seras déjà des nôtres.

– Je ne suis pas sûr d'avoir le temps, s'inquiète Mathis.

– Ce ne sera pas long, affirme Yuma.

De jeunes enfants se précipitent à l'intérieur d'une hutte recouverte de grandes feuilles séchées. Ils en ressortent aussi rapidement en tenant à la main des poteries remplies de peinture noire, rouge et blanche. Ils les déposent devant Yuma.

Mathis s'assoit en tailleur et accepte avec plaisir cette séance de maquillage.

– Tu es ici chez toi, insiste Zumo,

apparemment très heureux que sa fille ait trouvé un nouvel ami.

Sur le bateau de Christophe Colomb, l'ambiance est différente. Les hommes enfilent des casques et des plastrons en métal. Des rapières pendent déjà à leur ceinture, et Mina et Robin observent avec angoisse les épées que certains terminent d'affûter. Pendant ce temps, Christophe Colomb a ouvert l'armurerie devant laquelle de nombreux marins se rassemblent.

– Distribuez les arquebuses* et la poudre aux premiers de la file, ordonne-t-il. Que les autres prennent les arbalètes.

– Euh… êtes-vous certain que tout cela est nécessaire ? s'inquiète Mina.

– Nous ignorons ce que nous découvrirons sur cette terre, répond l'Amiral.

– La meilleure défense, c'est l'attaque, affirme Juan.

– Bien parlé ! approuvent plusieurs hommes en chargeant les armes.

– Ces forêts cachent sûrement des sauvages et des bêtes dangereuses, insiste le maître d'équipage.

Christophe Colomb sort sa longue-vue et observe la côte à présent toute proche.

– Je crois en effet apercevoir un village sur une colline, indique-t-il. Chargez les canons et dirigez-les vers le haut de la plage. Si une fois à terre j'agite ce mouchoir blanc, ouvrez le feu.

La nef s'arrête à une centaine de mètres du rivage, près des deux caravelles qui l'accompagnent. Les chaloupes sont aussitôt mises à l'eau.

Robin s'approche de Mina.

– J'ai l'impression qu'une guerre se prépare, lui confie-t-il à l'oreille.

10
Première rencontre

01 h 02

Un jeune Taïno vient de repérer la nef et les deux caravelles. Il arrive au village tout essoufflé pour annoncer la nouvelle.

– J'ai vu une barque géante, haute comme un cocotier, et deux autres plus petites ! Et elles viennent vers la plage !

– Ha ! Ha ! s'esclaffe Zumo. Tu nous fais une blague, mais ça ne prend pas.

– C'est la vérité ! proteste le garçon. Il y a même des hommes à l'intérieur !

Les Taïnos se moquent encore de lui... mais, quand ils s'approchent de l'entrée du village, ils aperçoivent aussi, du haut de leur colline, ces drôles d'embarcations plantées de grands bâtons. Ils n'en croient pas leurs yeux.

– Je vous l'avais bien dit ! se réjouit le jeune garçon en bombant le torse.

Cette fois, tous le regardent avec respect.

– Allons voir ces barques de plus près, déclare Zumo.

Sans attendre, les Taïnos se réunissent pour descendre vers la plage en cortège.

Mathis se retrouve très vite seul dans le village avec Yuma qui finit de le maquiller.

– J'ai terminé, annonce-t-elle. Et tu es… très beau.

Mathis, toujours sensible aux compliments, ne peut s'empêcher d'esquisser un sourire.

– Toi aussi, tu es très belle, chuchote-t-il à Yuma.

Elle lui retourne un regard éclatant et le dévisage un long moment.

– On va voir ce que font les autres ? propose Mathis, finalement un peu gêné.

Il se lève et distingue lui aussi les navires.

«Ce sont sûrement ceux de Christophe Colomb. Pourvu que Mina et Robin soient à bord de l'un d'eux», songe-t-il.

Avec Yuma, il retrouve les Taïnos qui se sont arrêtés en voyant des hommes mettre des barques à l'eau. Zumo s'empare des crânes disposés à l'entrée du village, aussitôt imité par les autres villageois.

– Nous allons présenter les étrangers à nos ancêtres, explique-t-il à Mathis.

– Euh... c'est vraiment indispensable? s'inquiète le garçon.

– Bien sûr, lui répond Yuma. Les anciens seraient très déçus de ne pas participer à ce grand moment.

Mathis doute que ce soit une bonne idée, mais il ne voit pas quel argument avancer pour faire changer d'avis les Taïnos...

Mina et Robin sont montés dans la chaloupe qui a quitté la nef. Christophe Colomb se tient debout, à la proue. Juan est également avec eux, visiblement impatient, comme tous les hommes à bord, de toucher terre.

– Souquez ferme ! ordonne l'Amiral.

Ses soldats rament avec force. La mer est calme et la chaloupe s'échoue bientôt sur le sable. Christophe Colomb est le premier à débarquer, un étendard royal à la main. Il s'apprête à prononcer quelques paroles solennelles pour marquer l'appartenance de ce territoire à la couronne d'Espagne... quand une bonne cinquantaine de Taïnos jaillissent de la forêt. Ils courent vers lui en poussant des cris et en brandissant des crânes !

– Soldats ! En joue ! commande aussitôt l'amiral.

Les hommes s'alignent sur la plage et arment leurs arquebuses, prêts à tirer, tandis que Christophe Colomb porte la main à sa poche pour sortir son mouchoir blanc...

11
Taïnos en danger!

00 h 50

Mathis est en tête de cortège avec Yuma et son père. En voyant les Espagnols pointer leurs armes vers eux, les Taïnos ne prennent pas peur, ignorant qu'ils sont en danger.

« Je dois absolument les arrêter », songe Mathis.

Au coude à coude avec Zumo, il crochète sa cheville d'un habile coup de pied. Le croc-en-jambe déséquilibre le père de Yuma qui effectue un spectaculaire vol plané, expédiant dans les airs le crâne qu'il tenait! Le chef atterrit lourdement sur le sable.

– Arrêtez ! s'écrie aussitôt Mathis. Zumo est blessé !

Les Taïnos stoppent leur course et se rassemblent autour de leur chef. Celui-ci, à plat ventre, secoue la tête pour reprendre ses esprits. Yuma, à qui rien n'a échappé, se rapproche de Mathis.

– Pourquoi as-tu fait un croche-pied à mon père ? chuchote-t-elle.

– Pour sauver ton peuple, se justifie Mathis. Je t'en prie, crois-moi. Les hommes blancs allaient vous tuer. Empêche ton père d'avancer pendant que je vais leur parler.

Yuma acquiesce.

– J'ai confiance en toi, murmure-t-elle à Mathis.

Elle effleure la main du jeune garçon, puis se faufile près de son père.

– Ne bouge pas, papa. Un mauvais esprit t'a fait trébucher. Je l'ai vu. Laisse-moi le chasser avant de te relever.

Le chef, affolé, obéit volontiers à sa fille. Chez les Taïnos, on ne plaisante pas avec les esprits !

Pendant ce temps, Mathis quitte le groupe et se dirige vers les Espagnols. À côté de Christophe Colomb, il aperçoit Mina et Robin. Soulagé de les retrouver, il leur adresse un signe de la main auquel ils ne répondent pas.

— Ce sauvage semble vous connaître, remarque l'amiral.

— C'est impossible, rétorque Mina.

Mais soudain, sous le maquillage de couleur, elle reconnaît son ami.

— Amiral ! Ne tirez pas ! s'écrie-t-elle. Surtout, ne tirez pas !

— Il me paraît moins menaçant que ses congénères, admet Colomb. J'accepte de lui laisser une chance.

Et il ordonne aux soldats de baisser leurs armes.

Mathis pousse un soupir de soulagement. Il s'approche prudemment et s'adresse à l'amiral.

— Les Taïnos ne vous feront aucun mal, jure-t-il. Ils veulent simplement vous souhaiter la bienvenue à leur façon.

– Mais tu parles parfaitement notre langue ! s'étonne Colomb.

– Vous avez raison, amiral, intervient Mina. À présent, je reconnais ce garçon. Il s'appelle Mathis et il était avec nous lors du naufrage. J'imagine qu'il s'est s'échoué ici.

Mathis confirme aussitôt son récit.

– Les Taïnos m'ont recueilli. Et ne vous fiez pas aux apparences, ils sont parfaitement pacifiques.

– Et ces crânes ? questionne l'amiral.

Mathis explique les croyances liées à ces ossements et les bonnes intentions des Taïnos.

– Tu comprends aussi leur langue ? demande Colomb.

– J'ai eu le temps d'apprendre quelques mots et je peux vous servir d'interprète.

– J'imagine que le langage de ces… euh… Indiens, appelons-les ainsi puisque nous sommes aux Indes, n'est pas très élaboré.

– Mais on n'est pas aux Indes, chuchote Robin. On est en Amérique !

– Chut ! lui retourne Mina. On ne doit pas changer le cours de l'Histoire.

— Alors, allons faire connaissance avec ces Indiens, propose le navigateur.

Mais il demeure visiblement soucieux. Il prend Mathis par les épaules et l'entraîne un peu à l'écart :

— Ainsi, tu es arrivé ici avant moi, lui dit-il à mi-voix.

— C'est exact, Amiral.

— Euh… ton histoire de naufrage et de rencontre avec les Indiens pourrait-elle rester entre nous ? Officiellement, j'aimerais être le premier navigateur à avoir posé le pied sur cette terre.

— Personne n'en saura rien, promet Mathis. Vous avez ma parole.

Satisfait de cette réponse, Christophe Colomb retrouve alors le sourire.

12
Un bijou exceptionnel

00 h 42

En voyant les hommes blancs s'avancer tranquillement avec Mathis, Yuma devine qu'elle peut rendre la liberté à son père. Elle agite les mains encore une fois au-dessus de son corps et lui assure que le mauvais esprit est parti. Les Taïnos félicitent la jeune fille et Zumo, soulagé, se relève. Il se saisit du crâne qu'il a laissé tomber, avant de rejoindre Christophe Colomb.

– Sois le bienvenu, Homme qui vient de l'océan, dit-il en le serrant dans ses bras.

L'amiral écourte son étreinte, trop familière

à son goût, mais il est sensible à ces mots d'accueil traduits par Mathis.

– Je suis également heureux de vous rencontrer, grand chef. Mes marins et moi arrivons en effet d'un pays très lointain. Nous sommes les représentants de la couronne espagnole.

Colomb brandit l'étendard de ses souverains qu'il plante dans le sable. Par ce geste, il déclare prendre possession de ce lieu au nom d'Isabelle la Catholique et de Ferdinand d'Aragon*.

– Je baptise cette nouvelle terre espagnole du nom du Christ : San Salvador, le Saint Sauveur ! proclame-t-il.

– Nous, nous appelons cet endroit Guanahani, s'amuse le chef. Mais tu peux le nommer comme cela te plaît.

– San Salvador, répète Colomb. J'en suis à présent le vice-roi et gouverneur général.

– C'est bien, approuve Zumo. Et moi, je reste le chef, ainsi, il n'y aura pas de jaloux.

Mina et Robin, eux, sont choqués par l'attitude du navigateur.

– Il se comporte comme s'il était chez lui, remarque le jeune garçon.

– Tu as raison, mais n'oublie pas qu'il est ici pour conquérir une terre, rappelle Mina.

Satisfait par la bonne volonté des Taïnos, Christophe Colomb décide de se montrer aimable envers ces Indiens qu'il semble finalement réellement apprécier. Il envoie Mina et Robin chercher un coffre dans la chaloupe.

– Zumo, annonce-t-il, j'ai des cadeaux pour vous.

Sitôt les deux enfants revenus, l'amiral retire du coffre des vêtements, des étoffes et des miroirs qu'il remet aux Indiens. Les Taïnos s'extasient devant ces présents qui sortent de l'ordinaire. Mais Zumo ne veut pas être en reste et il cherche une idée d'offrande digne de cette rencontre exceptionnelle. Il inspecte avec minutie les nombreux colliers qui ornent son cou et saisit un lacet de cuir au bout duquel pend un anneau en or particulièrement imposant. Des signes y sont gravés sur toute la circonférence. Mina et Robin échangent un clin d'œil : l'objet qu'ils doivent scanner pour réussir leur mission se trouve à portée de main.

– Voici un cadeau pour sceller notre amitié, Homme qui vient de l'océan, déclare Zumo. Il te protégera des mauvais sorts et des maladies.

Il remet l'anneau à Christophe Colomb qui ouvre des yeux aussi ronds que le bijou.

– C'est de l'or! murmurent les marins autour de lui. De l'or pur!

D'un regard sévère, l'amiral les fait taire.

13
De l'or !

00 h 31

Les Taïnos et les Espagnols remontent tranquillement vers le village des Indiens. Après avoir longuement inspecté l'anneau, Christophe Colomb le glisse dans sa poche et il s'adresse à Zumo par l'intermédiaire de Mathis :

– Ce métal jaune est magnifique. J'aimerais savoir si l'on peut en trouver dans la région.

– Bien sûr, répond le chef des Taïnos. Je peux te montrer où nous nous en procurons.

– J'en serais ravi, assure l'amiral.

– Cet or appartient aux Indiens, intervient Robin.

– Tout ce qui est ici appartient à la couronne d'Espagne, corrige le navigateur. Y compris ces Indiens fort sympathiques et coopératifs.

– S'ils n'acceptaient pas ce que vous leur demandez, vous les tueriez ?

– Je préfère les solutions diplomatiques, mais s'ils nous avaient attaqués, nous leur aurions offert davantage de plomb et de fer que d'étoffe !

La colère envahit Robin et il dirait bien à Colomb ce qu'il pense de sa façon d'agir. Mais il se rappelle qu'il doit avant tout réussir sa mission. Il repère le lacet en cuir qui dépasse de la poche de Christophe Colomb et cherche un moyen de détourner l'attention de tous. Il n'est pas long à échafauder un plan.

– Oh ! Regardez ces oiseaux colorés ! lance-t-il en désignant un groupe de perroquets vert émeraude perchés dans un arbre.

– Ils sont magnifiques ! s'extasie l'amiral. Nous devons absolument en rapporter en Espagne.

– Je m'en occupe ! assure un marin en pointant son arquebuse vers les oiseaux.

Il appuie aussitôt sur la détente et rate heureusement sa cible. Mais la détonation n'affole pas seulement les Indiens ; d'innombrables oiseaux, habitués à la tranquillité de l'île, s'envolent au-dessus de la forêt. Le ciel devient multicolore !

Christophe Colomb et ses marins lèvent la tête, fascinés par ce spectacle.

Robin saisit cette chance : il tire sur le lacet et fait disparaître l'anneau dans sa propre poche.

– Éloignons-nous, glisse-t-il à l'oreille de Mina.

Cette dernière fait signe à Mathis de la suivre et le trio s'écarte du groupe pendant que Christophe Colomb réprimande son soldat pour avoir effrayé les Indiens.

– J'ai parlé de capturer un oiseau, pas de le transformer en passoire !

– Je croyais bien faire, amiral, se justifie le soldat.

Un autre marin, surpris de voir les Taïnos

trembler de la tête aux pieds, s'approche d'eux avec son arquebuse.

– Ce n'est pas dangereux, assure-t-il. Il suffit de ne pas se trouver du mauvais côté.

Et, pour démontrer l'exactitude de ses propos, il tire en l'air ! Cette fois, les pauvres Indiens se jettent à terre, les mains sur la tête.

– Crétin ! s'emporte Christophe Colomb. Posez tous ces arquebuses ! C'est un ordre !

En temps normal, Juan s'amuserait d'une telle situation. Mais, en ce moment, il ne s'intéresse ni aux hommes sermonnés par l'amiral, ni aux Taïnos terrifiés. Il observe les trois naufragés qui se dirigent vers la sortie du village avec l'évidente volonté de passer inaperçus.

– Ces trois-là préparent un mauvais coup, marmonne-t-il.

Bien décidé à redorer son blason auprès de Christophe Colomb, il laisse l'amiral passer sa colère sur les marins et suit le trio.

14
Au voleur!

00 h 22

– Installons-nous derrière cette case, indique Robin.

Mathis et Mina entourent leur ami pendant qu'il sort l'anneau d'or de sa poche.

– Ouah! s'émerveille Mina. Il est magnifique!

Mathis, lui, n'en croit pas ses yeux:

– Tu as réussi à le voler à Christophe Colomb!

– Robin s'est découvert une vocation de pickpocket, plaisante Mina.

Son copain positionne l'anneau devant le

GTS. Le bracelet émet aussitôt un signal sonore… quand une ombre se dessine sur le sol. Les trois aventuriers relèvent la tête : Juan se tient face à eux, les poings sur les hanches.

– Bande de voleurs ! lance-t-il d'une voix menaçante. Vous finirez aux fers !

Surpris, le trio reste sans réaction. L'homme sort un couteau d'un étui fixé à sa ceinture et s'avance vers Robin. La lame brille au soleil et un sourire mauvais traverse le visage de Juan.

– Je vais récupérer cet anneau, promet le marin, et aussi la main qui l'a volé !

C'est alors que Yuma bondit sur son dos, tel un félin. Les combattants roulent à terre dans un nuage de poussière, d'où la jeune Indienne émerge la première. Juan reste au sol et son couteau est à présent entre les mains de Yuma. Elle s'en débarrasse dans un buisson.

– Suivez-moi, lance-t-elle.

– On peut lui faire confiance, affirme Mathis. Venez !

L'Indienne entraîne le trio à l'extérieur du village, sur un chemin qui s'enfonce dans la forêt. Très vite, le soleil disparaît, masqué derrière les feuillages.

Juan secoue la tête. Il serait incapable d'expliquer ce qui s'est passé. Est-ce un animal qui a bondi sur lui ? Il l'ignore. En revanche, il sait que les trois naufragés ont pris la fuite et qu'ils ont emporté avec eux le cadeau reçu par Colomb. Encore sonné, il se relève tout de même et file rejoindre les Espagnols en titubant.

– Amiral ! Amiral ! appelle-t-il. On vous a volé votre anneau !

En entendant son maître d'équipage, Colomb porte la main à sa poche.

– M… mais c'est la vérité ! s'exclame-t-il.

– Ce sont les naufragés qui ont fait le coup, lui apprend Juan en se présentant devant lui. Et l'Indien qui vous servait d'interprète est avec eux.

Les yeux de l'amiral se remplissent de colère.

– Laissez-moi m'en occuper, propose Juan. Je vous promets de les rattraper.

– Accordé ! décide Colomb. Prends cinq hommes armés avec toi et rapporte-moi cet anneau.

– Et les voleurs ?

– Réserve-leur le sort qu'ils méritent !

Un sourire féroce se dessine sur le visage de Juan.

Un peu plus loin dans la forêt, Yuma s'arrête et se tourne vers Mathis et ses amis.

– Pourquoi avez-vous volé l'anneau d'or ?

Mathis reprend son souffle. La jeune Indienne vient de leur sauver la vie et il n'a pas envie de lui mentir.

— Nous sommes originaires d'une région très lointaine, explique-t-il. Et nous avons besoin de cet objet pour y retourner.

— Tu veux rentrer chez toi ? semble regretter la jeune Taïnos.

— Oui, avoue Mathis. C'est ce que je souhaite.

— Alors je vais t'aider, car je t'aime beaucoup.

La franchise de Yuma touche le garçon… et fait sourire ses deux amis.

— Au lieu de ricaner dans mon dos, ronchonne Mathis, vous devriez scanner l'anneau.

— Devant Yuma ? s'étonne Mina. Je sais que tu l'aimes beaucoup, mais je doute que ce soit une bonne idée.

— Il souhaite peut-être qu'elle vienne avec nous dans le présent, pouffe Robin.

— Elle va découvrir des tas de choses inconnues avec les Espagnols, réplique Mathis. Qu'elle voie le GTS ne changera rien, et nous pourrons lui remettre l'anneau afin qu'elle le rende à Christophe Colomb.

– Ça, c'est un argument, admet Mina.

Robin sort de nouveau le bijou et le présente devant le GTS. Le bracelet s'active et un écran holographique apparaît.

> **Ah! J'espère que je ne serai pas interrompue, cette fois!**
> **Temps restant : 00 h 17 min 04 s.**

Yuma se fige sur place, les yeux fixés sur les rayons rouges qui commencent à balayer la surface de l'anneau. Soudain, des voix s'élèvent :

– Ils n'ont pas beaucoup d'avance !

– Ici ! Il y a des branches brisées. Ils ont dû passer par là !

Yuma pousse Robin, Mina et Mathis devant elle.

– Courez ! Droit devant ! Sinon, ils vont vous capturer !

> **Échec de la numérisation ! Grrrr !**
> **Temps restant : 00 h 16 min 38 s.**

15
Dangers dans la mangrove

00 h 15

– Où allons-nous ? s'inquiète Mathis.
– Nous redescendons vers la côte pour traverser la mangrove*, lui indique Yuma. C'est un endroit où il est facile de se perdre. Nous avons une chance d'y semer les hommes blancs.

La voix du maître d'équipage résonne derrière eux :
– Ils sont par ici ! Je les entends !

Les quatre enfants accélèrent l'allure. Derrière la jeune Indienne qui leur ouvre la voie, ils quittent bientôt le chemin. Ils avancent au milieu d'une végétation dense avant de s'enfoncer dans une forêt de palétuviers. Les arbres qui poussent en bordure de mer s'élèvent au-dessus du petit groupe, formant un toit végétal. Les racines, elles, s'entrelacent comme un tissage désordonné qui maintient les troncs hors de l'eau salée.

– Attention où vous mettez les pieds, prévient Yuma.

Mina et ses amis ont l'impression de marcher sur un filet tendu au-dessus de l'eau. Des singes, très à leur aise dans cet enchevêtrement végétal, s'éloignent à leur passage. Mina veut prendre exemple sur eux et s'accroche à une liane qui pend d'un arbre.

– Aaaaah ! hurle-t-elle en sentant le corps froid d'un serpent.

La liane prend vie et siffle au-dessus d'elle. Elle recule, perd l'équilibre, heurte Robin qui bascule à son tour. Mina termine à plat ventre sur les racines des palétuviers. Robin, lui, atterrit dans l'eau !

– L… le serpent ! bafouille Mathis. Il descend de l'arbre !

Le reptile mesure au moins trois mètres et glisse avec aisance, les yeux fixés sur Mina. Il s'avance vers elle en agitant sa langue à deux pointes.

– Relève-toi! crie Mathis à son amie. Vite!

Mais Mina, hypnotisée par l'animal, ne bouge pas. Le serpent ouvre sa gueule à quelques centimètres de son visage… et s'effondre. Une fléchette lui a traversé la tête.

Yuma range tranquillement à sa ceinture la sarbacane qu'elle vient d'utiliser. Puis elle soulève le serpent mort et le jette à l'eau.

– Hé! proteste Robin. Je suis là!

Mathis l'aide à remonter sur les racines.

– Il faut repartir, indique Yuma. Les hommes blancs arrivent.

Le petit groupe reprend son avancée dans la mangrove. La progression est difficile et chaque pas demande beaucoup d'efforts et d'attention. La forêt s'ouvre bientôt sur un large marécage et c'est une vase peu accueillante qui s'étend maintenant devant les enfants.

– Nous devons traverser, annonce Yuma.

— Mais… on va s'enfoncer, s'écrie Mathis.

— Marchez exactement dans mes pas, commande l'Indienne.

Elle quitte les racines des arbres et s'engage dans la vasière. Elle marche sur un chemin invisible connu seulement des Taïnos. Ses pieds s'enfoncent dans la boue jusqu'à la cheville, mais pas plus haut. Mathis la suit avec application. Mina et Robin l'imitent, conscients que le moindre écart sera fatal.

— C'est très bien, les encourage Yuma. Continuez, nous y sommes presque.

Juan et ses hommes arrivent alors au bord du marécage.

— Tirez ! Tirez ! ordonne le maître d'équipage.

Les marins reprennent leurs arquebuses qu'ils portaient en bandoulière. Mais le temps qu'ils se mettent en position, les enfants ont rejoint l'autre côté du marécage. Ils remontent sur les racines des palétuviers et disparaissent dans la forêt quand les premiers coups de feu résonnent.

— Vite ! Poursuivons-les ! enrage Juan.

— Euh… on risque de s'enliser, signale un

marin prudent. On devrait contourner le marécage.

– S'ils sont passés par là, nous passerons aussi, s'entête le maître d'équipage. Suivez leurs traces.

Les Espagnols se lancent alors aux trousses des enfants, mais, sur ce sol humide, les empreintes de pas s'effacent vite.

– On a un problème, pressent l'homme en tête du cortège.

L'instant d'après, il s'enfonce jusqu'aux genoux.

– Au secours ! hurle-t-il, paniqué. Sortez-moi de là !

En voulant l'aider, un second marin s'envase à son tour.

– Rebroussons chemin tant que nos traces sont encore visibles ! s'affole un autre.

Juan lance des cordes aux deux hommes enlisés et les tire de ce piège en revenant sur ses pas avec les autres marins. Mais il doit abandonner la poursuite et lâche une bordée de jurons face à cet échec cuisant !

En l'entendant crier et pester de la sorte,

les quatre enfants devinent qu'ils sont à présent en sécurité.

– Arrêtons-nous un instant pour scanner l'anneau, propose Mathis. Ainsi, nous saurons où se trouve le point R.

Robin sort le bijou de sa poche.

– Heureusement, je ne l'ai pas perdu en tombant dans l'eau, se réjouit-il.

Il le présente devant le GTS... mais rien ne se passe.

– Il ne fonctionne plus, se désespère-t-il. Je crois qu'il n'est pas étanche.

– Si on ne peut pas scanner l'objet, s'exclame Mathis, on ne pourra jamais rentrer chez nous !

16
Panne de GTS

00 h 08

– Et si on allumait un feu pour sécher le GTS ? propose Mathis.
– Super idée, ironise Robin. Une fois grillé, il fonctionnera sûrement mieux.
– Qu'est-ce qu'il suggère, alors, Monsieur-gros-malin ?
– Il faut le démonter et le laisser sécher au soleil.
– Ben voyons ! Et tu as sans doute un tournevis dans la poche ? demande Mathis.
Mina intervient pour calmer les garçons.
– Ça m'étonnerait que mon grand-père ait

mis au point une machine à remonter le temps sans concevoir un GTS étanche.

Elle inspecte le bracelet et pousse un cri de joie.

— Regardez ! L'eau de mer s'est évaporée en laissant une fine pellicule de sel. Voilà pourquoi les capteurs du GTS ne fonctionnent plus.

— Il faut de l'eau douce pour le rincer, approuve Robin.

— Je te rappelle qu'on est au bord de la mer, signale Mathis. Tu veux sans doute qu'on attende la prochaine averse ?

— J'ai plus simple, l'interrompt Mina.

Et elle crache sur le GTS avant de l'essuyer avec sa manche.

— Rose ne va pas apprécier, prédit Robin.

Le GTS grésille et se rallume.

> **Que s'est-il passé ? Pourquoi le contact a-t-il été coupé ?**
> **Temps restant : 00 h 06 min 47 s.**

— Sans doute une interférence, Rose, invente

Robin. Mais vous pouvez scanner l'anneau, à présent.

Sous le regard attentif et un peu angoissé de Yuma, le bracelet émet plusieurs rayons rouges qui balaient la surface de l'objet. L'opération ne dure que quelques secondes.

> **Numérisation réussie. Rendez-vous au point R : maison des Prières.**
> **Temps restant : 00 h 06 min 21 s.**

Un plan apparaît sur l'écran holographique.
– La maison des Prières est tout près d'ici, note Mathis. Yuma, peux-tu nous y conduire ?

La jeune Indienne continue d'observer le GTS avec fascination.

– Euh… la maison des Prières se trouve sur le territoire des Mayanos, se reprend-elle. Je n'ai pas le droit d'y pénétrer, mais je peux vous montrer comment quitter la mangrove.

– C'est très gentil à toi, la remercie Robin en lui remettant l'anneau. Tu le redonneras à l'amiral Colomb de notre part.

– Tu dois trouver tout ce que nous faisons très étrange, ajoute Mina.

– J'ai confiance en vous, dit Yuma en attachant le bijou en or à son cou. Maintenant, venez.

Quelques instants plus tard, le groupe retrouve le soleil et la terre ferme. Devant eux, un chemin traverse une petite plaine couverte d'herbes hautes, avant de descendre vers la vallée.

– Restez sur ce sentier et vous verrez bientôt la maison des Prières, explique Yuma. Mais évitez les Mayanos, car ce sont des guerriers qui n'aiment pas les étrangers.

– Nous ferons attention, promet Mina en prenant la jeune Indienne dans ses bras. Nous te remercions de tout cœur.

Robin la salue d'un geste de la main. Mathis veut suivre son exemple mais, cette fois, c'est Yuma qui le serre contre elle.

– J'espère te revoir bientôt, bel inconnu.

– Ben… c'est-à-dire… je vais être très occupé ces prochains jours, bafouille Mathis.

– Je t'attendrai, promet Yuma.

Et elle l'embrasse sur la bouche !

– Hmmmm ! proteste le garçon en roulant des yeux dans tous les sens.

Robin et Mina éclatent de rire. Puis Yuma libère Mathis et disparaît en courant vers la mangrove.

– Mon pote, tu es un vrai tombeur ! se moque Robin.

– Oui, bon, dépêchons-nous de rejoindre le point R si on ne veut pas rester bloqués dans cette époque.

– Ça ne déplairait pas à Yuma, commente Mina malicieusement.

– Alors, vous venez ? s'énerve Mathis.

17
Chez les Mayanos

00 h 04

Le trio traverse la plaine en courant. Aux abords de la vallée, en contrebas, une grande hutte rectangulaire apparaît. Elle est isolée et son emplacement correspond à celui indiqué sur le plan.

— La maison des Prières, se réjouit Robin.

Mais quatre silhouettes se dessinent près de la cabane. En file indienne, elles remontent vers les enfants.

— Des Mayanos, chuchote Mina qui entraîne ses amis en arrière. Cachons-nous pour les laisser passer.

– Inutile de perdre du temps, objecte Mathis. Ces Indiens m'ont l'air tout à fait sympathiques. Ils ont de l'allure avec leurs belles plumes colorées accrochées à la ceinture.

– Yuma nous a prévenus qu'ils étaient dangereux, rappelle Robin.

– C'est certainement une jalousie entre tribus voisines, estime son copain. Laissez-moi faire et nous arriverons plus vite à la maison des Prières.

Pour couper court aux protestations de ses camarades, Mathis descend le premier dans la vallée. Robin et Mina n'ont pas le temps de le retenir, alors ils se résignent à le suivre. Les Indiens repèrent aussitôt le trio.

– Regardez, ils nous sourient, se réjouit Mathis. Hé ho! Bonjour les amis!

– Ils courent vers nous! s'affole Robin.

– Ils sont pressés de nous rencontrer, affirme Mathis.

– Ils ont de magnifiques plumes mais aussi de beaux arcs! remarque Mina.

– Et des flèches! ajoute Robin.

– Sauve qui peut ! hurle Mathis en revenant sur ses pas.

Ses amis l'imitent. De retour au sommet de la vallée, dès que le trio n'est plus visible des Indiens, Mina arrête les garçons. Elle désigne un arbre mort tombé dans l'herbe haute.

– Couchons-nous derrière ce tronc. Les Mayanos ne nous verront pas.

Le trio saute au-dessus de l'arbre et s'allonge à même le sol, le cœur battant. Les enfants retiennent leur souffle quand, une poignée de secondes plus tard, les quatre Indiens parviennent en haut de la vallée.

– Les intrus ont dû traverser la plaine, dit l'un d'eux.

– Pourtant, je ne les vois pas, répond un autre.

– Ils se cachent sûrement dans les herbes, reprend le premier. Allons les débusquer !

Les Mayanos repartent aussitôt, l'arc à la main, prêts à tirer. Ils s'éloignent de l'arbre mort pour inspecter les alentours.

– Ils nous tournent le dos, prévient Mina. Profitons-en pour rejoindre le point R.

Les trois amis quittent discrètement leur cachette et disparaissent dans la vallée qu'ils dévalent à toute vitesse.

– Hé! Hé! On les a bien eus! ricane Mathis.

Une flèche siffle alors au-dessus de sa tête avant de se figer dans un bananier. Mina se retourne et constate que les Indiens viennent de se lancer à leur poursuite.

– Plus qu'une minute, annonce Robin en consultant le GTS.

– Ça tombe bien, on est super pressés! crie Mathis en le dépassant.

La Maison des Prières est encore à une centaine de mètres. Heureusement, le chemin qui serpente à travers la végétation ne permet plus aux Mayanos d'utiliser leurs flèches. Pour l'instant, ils peuvent seulement poursuivre les enfants.

– Robin! Continue, ne ralentis pas! s'alarme Mina.

Voyant qu'il est à bout de force, son amie lui attrape le poignet. Mathis est déjà arrivé à la maison des Prières et il encourage ses camarades à sa manière.

– Dépêchez-vous, espèces de limaces ! Les Indiens gagnent du terrain !

Les Mayanos viennent en effet d'apparaître derrière ses copains.

— Tiens bon ! lance Mina à Robin. On y est presque !

Mathis, une grosse branche à la main, attend ses amis sur le seuil de la hutte. Il s'écarte pour les laisser entrer et referme immédiatement la porte après lui. Trois flèches tirées de l'extérieur la transpercent en partie. Mathis bloque l'ouverture avec le bout de bois et se tourne vers Robin.

— Combien de temps ?

— Encore seize secondes !

Seule une statue entourée de fleurs trône au milieu de la maison rectangulaire. Dans la pénombre, les enfants échangent un regard angoissé. Les Indiens commencent à forcer la porte. Mathis appuie dans l'autre sens pour les empêcher d'entrer.

— Je ne tiendrai pas longtemps, prévient-il.

— Neuf secondes.

— Pour une fois que nous sommes en avance ! se lamente Mina.

— Cinq, quatre, trois...

Mathis lutte de toutes ses forces, mais la branche est sur le point de céder.

— Le cercle ! s'écrie Mina.

— Allez-y ! hurle Mathis.

Il résiste à une nouvelle poussée des Mayanos pendant que Mina et Robin sautent dans le cercle holographique apparu à côté de la statue. Puis Mathis lâche prise. La branche se casse aussitôt et la porte s'ouvre. Deux Indiens se précipitent pour attraper le jeune garçon… mais celui-ci bondit dans le filtre temporel et disparaît sous leurs yeux.

18
Rose se fâche

Robin, Mina et Mathis reprennent leur souffle au centre du laboratoire secret de Théodore Champollion. Le cercle holographique se referme sous leurs pieds.

— Cette aventure m'a épuisée ! avoue Mina.

— Mais pourquoi avons-nous été séparés ? demande Robin.

— **Mathis a voulu me confier ceci avant de partir**, répond Rose.

Le MP3 de Dark apparaît au bout de la tige télescopique.

— J'avais peur de le perdre, se justifie Mathis en reprenant son bien.

— **Oui, mais tu as failli rater le départ.**

Robin en profite pour remettre le GTS en place.

— Il faudra le nettoyer un peu, précise-t-il à l'intention de Rose.

La machine n'est pas longue à analyser la substance dont il reste encore des traces sur le bracelet.

— **De la salive !** s'emporte-t-elle. **Qui a craché sur le GTS ?**

— Cette mission était très difficile, on en a bavé, plaisante Mathis.

Pendant que Rose continue de ronchonner, une trappe s'ouvre au plafond. Retenu par une pince articulée, un présentoir holographique rejoint le sol. Une lumière blanche s'en échappe et irradie la pièce. L'anneau d'or apparaît en trois dimensions, image parfaitement conforme à l'objet offert à Christophe Colomb par les Taïnos.

Mina soulève le présentoir et, après avoir salué Rose, elle quitte le laboratoire avec les garçons en emportant ce nouveau trophée.

— **C'est ça, à la prochaine !** lance la machine, toujours très contrariée.

Et elle referme le passage secret.

Une fois sortis du bureau de Théodore Champollion, les enfants ne sont pas vraiment surpris de se trouver nez à nez avec Hippolyte, le vieux gardien. Mina lui remet le présentoir où l'on peut maintenant admirer l'incomparable anneau virtuel, qui semble flotter dans les airs.

– S'il était parmi nous, Théodore serait fier de vous, les félicite le gardien.

– Il sera encore plus fier le jour où je le ramènerai dans le présent.

Mina sert la main d'Hippolyte, puis elle sort du musée en compagnie de ses deux amis.

Le trio retrouve le monde moderne, sans Indiens ni navigateur.

– Et si on s'offrait une partie de bowling pour se détendre ? propose Robin.

– Super idée ! approuvent en chœur Mina et Mathis.

Les trois copains se frappent dans les mains, quand ils aperçoivent un garçon habillé tout en noir qui traverse le parc.

—Ce ne serait pas Dark ? demande Mina.

—Avec son look, on peut difficilement se tromper, plaisante Robin.

Mathis le réprimande immédiatement.

—Il ne faut pas juger les gens à leur apparence, dit-il d'un ton professoral.

—C'est toi qui… commence Mina.

—J'ai tiré certaines leçons de notre aventure, la coupe Mathis. À présent, je vois les choses différemment.

Pour le prouver, il interpelle Dark. Ce dernier, d'abord surpris, rejoint le trio.

—Tu veux venir avec nous au bowling ? lui demande Mathis.

—Bien sûr ! se réjouit Dark.

—Il faudra changer de chaussures, le prévient Robin. Mais je ne suis pas certain qu'ils en aient avec des têtes de mort.

—Ne t'inquiète pas, le rassure Dark. J'ai choisi ce style car je suis fan de plusieurs groupes gothiques… mais je porte aussi un pyjama bleu ciel ! Et j'ai même découvert une ou deux chansons écoutables sur le MP3 de Mathis !

Robin et ses amis éclatent de rire.

– Finalement, il est drôlement sympa, ce garçon, chuchote Mina à l'oreille de Mathis.
– Hé! Je l'ai toujours dit! assure son ami.
– Menteur! s'offusque Mina.

Mathis sourit, puis il pose sa main sur l'épaule de Dark avant d'entraîner tout le monde vers le bowling.

LES MOTS DE ROSE

Des milliards d'informations sont stockées dans mon cerveau électronique. En voici quelques-unes que j'ai sélectionnées pour t'éclairer sur cette aventure :

ANNEAU

Hélas, on n'en a retrouvé aucune trace. Il a sans doute disparu lors du voyage retour de l'explorateur. Tu ne pourras le voir dans aucun musée... à part celui de Théodore, bien sûr !

ARQUEBUSE

Ce fusil ne pèse pas moins de neuf kilos. Il faut des soldats costauds pour utiliser ce genre d'arme. Pas question d'embarquer des gringalets à bord des navires !

CARTE

En 1492, Le GTS n'existe pas. Il faut se fier à des cartes maritimes incomplètes et parfois fausses. En effet, les cartes utilisées par Colomb ne présentent pas les bonnes distances entre l'Espagne et les Indes. Aussi le navigateur est-il persuadé qu'il est réalisable de franchir cette distance. Cela lui réserve de belles surprises !

GOYAVE

C'est l'un des nombreux fruits exotiques découverts en Amérique. On y trouve aussi le maïs, la tomate et la pomme de terre. Mais, au départ, les Européens refusent de manger cette dernière et la donnent uniquement à leurs cochons. Ils sont persuadés qu'elle transmet des maladies puisqu'elle pousse sous terre. Il faudra près de trois cents ans pour qu'ils acceptent de la consommer... et que les frites apparaissent enfin au menu !

INDES

Pour rejoindre les Indes plus rapidement, Christophe Colomb décide de passer par l'ouest, et d'éviter ainsi un long détour le long des côtes africaines. Il espère ainsi ouvrir une route commerciale. Cet itinéraire est jusqu'alors inconnu. Quand il touche enfin terre, il est donc persuadé d'être arrivé aux Indes et baptise ses habitants les Indiens ! Il meurt en 1506 en ignorant toujours avoir découvert l'Amérique.

ISABELLE LA CATHOLIQUE ET FERDINAND II D'ARAGON

Les navigateurs ont déjà des sponsors à l'époque. Colomb cherche d'abord à faire financer son expédition par le roi du Portugal. Il essuie un refus… et s'adresse alors aux souverains espagnols. La reine Isabelle est impressionnée par Colomb qui lui promet des navires chargés d'or et d'épices et elle va convaincre son époux de soutenir le navigateur. Les souverains espèrent tirer de grands bénéfices commerciaux de cette expédition.

MANGROVE

Elle est constituée de marais salés en partie recouverts par la mer et où poussent des palétuviers. Pour supporter le sel marin, ces arbres développent des racines aériennes et forment de véritables forêts sur pilotis ! Pour que leurs graines soient à l'abri de l'eau de mer, celles-ci germent directement sur l'arbre et se détachent ensuite. C'est donc un jeune palétuvier qui vient se planter dans la vase. Eh oui, les arbres sont très malins !

NEF, CARAVELLE

Colomb organise une expédition avec deux caravelles et une nef. Les deux frères Pinzón commandent chacun une des caravelles. Colomb embarque sur la nef. La caravelle, récemment inventée, présente de nombreux avantages : légère, longue et étroite, elle permet d'avancer à grande vitesse. La nef est la plus grande des embarcations. Elle est moins rapide. Son ancre mesure quatre mètres !

SABLIER

L'horloge existe déjà en 1492 mais elle est trop encombrante à bord d'un bateau. On lui préfère le sablier qu'un marin est chargé de retourner toutes les trente minutes. Et il n'a pas intérêt à s'endormir !

SUPERSTITIEUX

Les marins sont extrêmement superstitieux. Par exemple, les femmes ne sont pas les bienvenues sur les bateaux, car ils sont persuadés qu'elles apportent le malheur. Personne ne doit également prononcer le mot « lapin » tant ce rongeur est redouté à bord.

GRAND CONCOURS OPÉRATION TRIO

DU 1ᴱᴿ MARS AU 30 JUIN 2012

Toi aussi, tu rêves de voyager dans le temps ?
Tu veux aider Mina à retrouver son grand-père ?

Alors rejoins-nous vite sur

WWW.OPERATION-TRIO.FR

pour tenter de devenir le héros du prochain tome
de la série aux côtés de Mina, Mathis et Robin !

À bientôt !

Composition : Catherine Enault

© Éditions Nathan (Paris, France), 2012
Loi n° 49-956 du 16 juillet 1949
sur les publications destinées à la jeunesse
ISBN : 978-2-09-253862-3

N° d'éditeur : 10181762 – Dépôt légal : mars 2012
Imprimé en France par Hérissey à Évreux (Eure) – N° d'imprimeur : 118158

FREE AT LAST
THE U.S. CIVIL RIGHTS MOVEMENT

"I Have A Dream": The August, 1963 March on Washington for Jobs and Freedom was the largest political demonstration the nation had ever seen. Crowds gathered before the Lincoln Memorial and around the Washington Monument reflection pool heard Dr. Martin Luther King Jr. offer perhaps the finest oration ever delivered by an American.

CONTENTS

1

Slavery Spreads to America   3

A Global Phenomenon Transplanted to America
Slavery Takes Hold
Slave Life and Institutions
Family Bonds
SPOTLIGHT: The Genius of the Black Church

2

"Three-Fifths of Other Persons:" A Promise Deferred   8

A Land of Liberty?
The Pen of Frederick Douglass
The Underground Railroad
By the Sword
The Rebellious John Brown
The American Civil War
SPOTLIGHT: Black Soldiers in the Civil War

3

"Separate but Equal:" African Americans Respond to the Failure of Reconstruction   18

Congressional Reconstruction
Temporary Gains ... and Reverses
The Advent of "Jim Crow"
Booker T. Washington: The Quest for Economic Independence
W.E.B. Du Bois: The Push for Political Agitation
SPOTLIGHT: Marcus Garvey: Another Path

4

Charles Hamilton Houston and Thurgood Marshall Launch the Legal Challenge to Segregation   26

Charles Hamilton Houston: The Man Who Killed Jim Crow
Thurgood Marshall: Mr. Civil Rights
The *Brown* Decision
SPOTLIGHT: Ralph Johnson Bunche: Scholar and Statesman
SPOTLIGHT: Jackie Robinson: Breaking the Color Barrier

5

"We Have a Movement"   35

"Tired of Giving In:" The Montgomery Bus Boycott
Sit-Ins
Freedom Rides
The Albany Movement
Arrest in Birmingham
Letter From Birmingham Jail
"We Have a Movement"
The March on Washington
SPOTLIGHT: Rosa Parks: Mother of the Civil Rights Movement
SPOTLIGHT: Civil Rights Workers: Death in Mississippi
SPOTLIGHT: Medgar Evers: Martyr of the Mississippi Movement

6

"It Cannot Continue:" Establishing Legal Equality   52

Changing Politics
Lyndon Baines Johnson
The Civil Rights Act of 1964
The Act's Powers
The Voting Rights Act of 1965: The Background
Bloody Sunday in Selma
The Selma-to-Montgomery March
The Voting Rights Act Enacted
What the Act Does
SPOTLIGHT: White Southerners' Reactions to the Civil Rights Movement

Epilogue   65

The Triumphs of the Civil Rights Movement

SLAVERY SPREADS TO AMERICA

Among the antiquities displayed at the United Nations headquarters in New York is a replica of the Cyrus Cylinder. Named for Cyrus the Great, ruler of the Persian Empire and conqueror of Babylonia, the document dates to about 539 B.C. Cyrus guaranteed to his subjects many of what we today call civil rights, among them freedom of religion and protection of personal property. Cyrus also abolished slavery, "a tradition," he asserted, that "should be exterminated the world over."

Throughout history, nations have varied in how broadly they define and how vigorously they defend their citizens' personal protections and privileges. The United States is a nation built on these civil rights, on the soaring ideals enshrined in its Declaration of Independence and the legal protections formalized in its Constitution, and most prominently, in the first 10 amendments to that Constitution, known collectively as the American people's Bill of Rights.

Yet one group of arrivals did not enjoy those rights and protections. Even as European immigrants found unprecedented economic opportunity and greater personal, political, and religious liberty in the New World, black Africans were transported there involuntarily, often in chains, to be sold as chattel slaves and compelled to labor for "masters," most commonly in the great agricultural plantations in the South.

This book recounts how those African-American slaves and their descendants struggled to win — both in law and in practice — the civil rights enjoyed by other Americans. It is a story of dignified persistence and struggle, a story that produced great heroes and heroines, and one that ultimately succeeded by forcing the majority of Americans to confront squarely the shameful gap between their universal principles of equality and justice and the inequality, injustice, and oppression faced by millions of their fellow citizens.

A Global Phenomenon Transplanted to America

Man has enslaved his fellow man since prehistoric times. While the conditions of servitude varied, slave labor was employed by the ancient Mesopotamian, Indian, and Chinese civilizations, in classical Greece and Rome, and in pre-Colombian America by the native Aztec, Inca, and Mayan empires. The Bible tells us that the Egyptians used Hebrew slaves and that the Hebrews, upon their exodus from Egypt, used slaves of their own. Early Christianity accepted the practice, as did Islam. North and East African Arabs enslaved black Africans, and Egypt and Syria enslaved Mediterranean Europeans, whom they captured or purchased from slave traders and typically employed to produce sugar. Many Native American tribal groups enslaved members of other tribes captured in war.

A number of factors combined to stimulate the Atlantic slave trade. The Ottoman conquest of Constantinople (now Istanbul) in 1453 disturbed trade patterns and deprived sweet-toothed Europeans of highly prized sugar. Led by the Portuguese, Europeans began to explore the West African coast and to purchase slaves from African slave traders. After Christopher Columbus's 1492 discovery of the New World, European colonizers imported large numbers of African slaves to work the land and, especially in the Caribbean, to

Enslaved Africans on the deck of the bark *Wildfire*, Key West, Florida, April 1860.

FREE AT LAST: THE U.S. CIVIL RIGHTS MOVEMENT 3

An 1823 drawing depicts slaves cutting sugar cane on the Caribbean island of Antigua.

cultivate sugar. Caribbean islands soon supplied some 80 to 90 percent of Western Europe's sugar demand.

It is difficult in today's world to understand the prominent role that crops such as sugar, tobacco, cotton, and spices once played in the world economy. In 1789, for example, the small colony of Saint Domingue (today's Haiti) accounted for about 40 percent of the value of all French foreign trade. The economic forces driving the Atlantic slave trade were powerful. In all, at least 10 million Africans endured the "middle passage." (The term refers to the Atlantic Ocean segment — the second and longest — of the triangular trade that sent textiles, rum, and manufactured goods to Africa, slaves to the Americas, and sugar, tobacco and cotton to Europe.) Most arrived in Portuguese Brazil, Spanish Latin America, and the various British and French Caribbean "sugar islands." Only about 6 percent of the enslaved Africans were brought to British North America. Even so, the African-American experience differed profoundly from those of the other immigrants who would found and expand the United States.

Slavery Takes Hold

The very first slaves in British North America arrived by accident. Twelve years after the 1607 founding of the first permanent British settlement, at Jamestown, Virginia, a privateer docked there with some "20 and odd Negros" it had captured from a Spanish ship in the Caribbean. The settlers purchased this "cargo," the original slaves in the future United States.

For the next 50 years, slaves were not a prominent source of labor in the fledgling Virginia colony. The landowning elites preferred to rely on "indentured" white labor. Under this arrangement, potential European immigrants signed an indenture, or contract, under which they borrowed from an employer the price of transportation to America. In return, they agreed to work several years to pay off that debt. During this period, the sociologist Orlando Patterson writes, relations between the races were relatively intimate. A small number of particularly resourceful blacks even obtained their freedom and prospered in their own right.

Beginning in the second half of the 17th century, however, both the price of slaves and the supply of immigrants willing to indenture themselves decreased. As slave labor became cheaper than indentured labor, slavery grew and spread. By 1770, African Americans comprised about 40 percent of the population in the southern colonies and a majority in South Carolina. (Slaves were also found in the northern colonies, but the slave population there never exceeded about 5 percent.) Faced with such a large, oppressed, and potentially rebellious minority, southern elites encouraged a hardening of social attitudes toward African Americans. The children of slave women were declared to be slaves. Masters were permitted to kill slaves in the course of punishing them. Perhaps most importantly, white Virginia elites began to promote anti-black racism as a means of dividing blacks from less wealthy white workers.

Most African-American slaves labored on farms that produced staple crops: tobacco in Maryland, Virginia, and North Carolina; rice in the Deep South. In 1793, the American inventor Eli Whitney produced the first cotton gin, a mechanical device that removed cotton seeds from the surrounding cotton fiber. This spurred a dramatic expansion in cotton cultivation throughout the Lower South, one that expanded westward through Alabama, Mississippi, and Louisiana and into Texas. About one million African-American slaves moved westward during the period 1790-1860, nearly twice the number carried to the United States from Africa.

Slave Life and Institutions

African-American slaves were compelled to work hard, and in some cases brutally hard. In some states, laws known as slave codes authorized terrible punishments for offending slaves. According to Virginia's 1705 slave code:

> All Negro, mulatto, and Indian slaves within this dominion ... shall be held to be real estate. If any slave resist his master ... correcting such slave, and shall happen to be killed in such correction ... the master shall be free of all punishment ... as if such accident never happened.

This code also required that slaves obtain written permission before leaving their plantation. It authorized whipping, branding, and maiming as punishment for even minor offenses. Some codes forbade teaching slaves how to read and write. In Georgia, the punishment for this offense was a fine and/or whipping if the guilty party were a "slave, Negro, or free person of color."

Although the lot of American slaves was harsh, they labored under material conditions by some measures comparable to those endured by many European workers and peasants of that era. But there was a difference. The slaves lacked their freedom.

Denial of fundamental human rights handicapped African-American political and economic progress, but slaves responded by creating institutions of their own, vibrant institutions on which the civil rights movement of the mid-20th century would later draw for sustenance and social capital. Earlier accounts often portrayed the slaves as infantilized objects "acted upon" by their white masters, but we now understand that many slave communities managed to carve out a measure of personal, cultural, and religious autonomy. "It was not that the slaves did not act like men," historian Eugene Genovese writes. "Rather, it was that they could not grasp their collective strength as a people and act like political men." Nevertheless, Genovese concludes that most slaves "found ways to develop and assert their manhood and womanhood despite the dangerous compromises forced upon them."

One way was the "black church." Over time, increasing numbers of African-American slaves embraced Christianity, typically denominations like Baptist and Methodist that prevailed among white southerners. Some masters feared that Christian tenets would undermine their justifications for slavery, but others encouraged their slaves to attend church, although in a separate, "blacks-only" section.

After exposure to Christianity, many slaves then established their own parallel, or underground, churches. These churches often blended Christianity with aspects of the slaves' former African religious cultures and beliefs. Religious services commonly incorporated shouting, dance, and the call-and-response interactions that would later feature prominently in the great sermons of Dr. Martin Luther King Jr. and other leading black preachers. The black church often emphasized different aspects of the Christian tradition than did southern white churches. Where the latter might interpret the biblical Curse of Ham ("a servant of servants shall he be unto his brethren") as justifying slavery, African-American services might instead emphasize the story of how Moses led the Israelites from bondage.

For African-American slaves, religion offered a measure of solace and hope. After the American Civil War brought an end to slavery, black churches and denominational organizations grew in membership, influence, and organizational strength, factors that would prove vital to the success of the civil rights movement.

Family Bonds

The slaves' tight family bonds would prove a similar source of strength. Slave masters could, and often did, split up families — literally selling members to other slave owners, splitting husband from wife, parents from children. But many slave families remained intact, and many scholars have noted the "remarkable stability, strength, and durability of the nuclear family under slavery." Slaves were typically housed as extended family units. Slave children, historian C. Vann Woodward writes, at least "were assured a childhood, one exempt from labor and degradation past the age when working-class children of England and France were condemned to mine and factory."

A drawing, circa 1860, depicts a black preacher addressing his mixed-race congregation on a South Carolina plantation.

The African-American family structure adapted to meet the challenges posed by slavery, and later by discrimination and economic inequality. Many black family units resembled extended clans rather than smaller, immediate families. Some were organized with strong females as central authority figures. Slaveholders sometimes encouraged these family ties, reasoning that the threat of breaking up a family helped undermine the threats of disobedience and rebellion.

Regardless, strong immediate and extended families helped ensure African-American survival. In the Caribbean colonies and in Brazil, slave mortality rates exceeded birth rates, but blacks in the United States reproduced at the same rate as the white population. By the 1770s, only one in five slaves in British North America had been born in Africa. Even after 1808, when the United States banned the importation of slaves, their numbers increased from 1.2 million to nearly 4 million on the eve of the Civil War in 1861.

Slavery brought Africans to America and deprived them of the freedoms enjoyed by Americans of European origin. But even in bondage, many African Americans developed strong family ties and faith-based institutions and laid a foundation upon which future generations could build a triumphant civil rights movement. The struggle for freedom and equality began long before Rosa Parks claimed a seat on the front of the bus, more than a century before Martin Luther King Jr. inspired Americans with his famous dream.

THE GENIUS OF THE BLACK CHURCH

African-American religious communities have contributed immensely to American society, not least by supplying much of the moral, political, and organizational foundation of the 20th-century civil rights movement and by shaping the thought of its leaders, Rosa Parks and the Reverend Martin Luther King Jr. among them.

Enslaved and free African-Americans formed their own congregations as early as the mid- to late 18th century. After emancipation, fully fledged denominations emerged. What we today call the "black church" encompasses seven major historic black denominations: African Methodist Episcopal (AME); African Methodist Episcopal Zion (AMEZ); Christian Methodist Episcopal (CME); the National Baptist Convention, USA, Incorporated; the National Baptist Convention of America, Unincorporated; the Progressive National Baptist Convention; and the Church of God in Christ.

These denominations emerged after the emancipation of the African-American slaves. They drew mainly on Methodist, Baptist, and Pentecostal traditions, but often featured ties to American Catholicism, Anglicanism, the United Methodist Church, and a host of other traditions.

The great gift, indeed genius, of African-American religious sensibility is its drive to forge a common identity. Black slaves from different parts of Africa were transported to America by means of the "middle passage" across the Atlantic. As slaves, they endured massive oppression. Against this background of diversity and social deprivation, African-American religious belief and practice afforded solace and the intellectual foundation for a successful means of solving deep-seated conflict: the techniques of civil disobedience and nonviolence. The black church also supplied black political activists with a powerful philosophy: to focus upon an ultimate solution for all rather than palliatives for a select few. The civil rights movement would adopt this policy — never to allow systemic oppression of any human identity. Its genius, then, was a natural overflow from African-American religious communities that sought to make sense of a tragic history and move toward a future, not just for themselves, but also for their nation and the world.

In short, while some form of resistance to slavery and then Jim Crow segregation probably was inevitable, the communal spirituality of the black church in the face of repression helped spawn a civil rights movement that sought its objectives by peaceful means.

Many of the powerful voices of the civil rights movement — King, of course, but also such powerful and significant figures as U.S. Representatives Barbara Jordan and John Lewis, the political activist and Baptist minister Jesse Jackson, and the gospel legend Mahalia Jackson — all were formed from their worship life in the black church. Indeed, King's role as chief articulator of civil rights reflects the direct relationship between African-American religious communities and the struggle for racial and social justice in the United States. The spiritual influence of African-American religious practice spread beyond this nation's shores, as global leaders such as Nelson Mandela and Archbishop Desmond Tutu learned from King how to embody a loving, inclusive African and Christian identity.

Today's African-American communal spirituality is as strong and engaged as ever. Black churches work to craft responses to contemporary challenges such as the spread of HIV/AIDS, the need to ameliorate poverty, and the disproportionate recidivism of imprisoned African Americans. The search toward common identity remains the foundation of such a spirituality, however. Through the election of the first African-American president and the increase of minorities in higher education, the journey toward common identity remains on course.

In sum, the black church helped African Americans survive the harshest forms of oppression and developed a revolutionary appeal for universal communal spirituality. The black church didn't just theorize about democracy, it practiced democracy. From its roots there flowered the civil rights movement — creative, inclusive, and nonviolent.

By **Michael Battle**
Ordained a priest by Archbishop Desmond Tutu, the Very Rev. Michael Battle is Provost and Canon Theologian of the Cathedral Center of St. Paul in the Episcopal Diocese of Los Angeles. His books include *The Black Church in America: African American Spirituality*.

2
"Three-Fifths of Other Persons"
A PROMISE DEFERRED

During the 19th and early 20th centuries, African Americans and their white allies employed many strategies as they fought to end slavery and then to secure legal equality for the "freedmen." Progress toward racial equality was destined to be slow, not least because slavery and oppression of blacks were among the sectional political compromises that undergirded national unity. The Civil War of 1861-1865 would end slavery in the United States, but once the conflict ended, northern political will to overcome white southern resistance to racial equality gradually ebbed. The imposition of the "Jim Crow" system of legal segregation throughout the South stifled black political progress. Nevertheless, African-American leaders continued to build the intellectual and institutional capital that would nourish the successful civil rights movements of the mid- to late 20th century.

Depiction of George Washington with his black field workers on his Mount Vernon, Virginia, estate, 1757.

A Land of Liberty?

Slavery divided Americans from their very first day of independence. As the South grew more dependent on a new staple crop — "King Cotton" — and on the slave-intensive plantations that cultivated it, the prospect of a clash with increasingly antislavery northern states grew. The young nation delayed that conflict with a series of moral evasions and political compromises.

The United States' Declaration of Independence (1776) includes stirring language on universal brotherhood: "We hold these Truths to be self-evident, that all Men are created equal, that they are endowed by their Creator with certain unalienable Rights, that among these are Life, Liberty, and the Pursuit of Happiness." And yet its principal draftsman, Thomas Jefferson, was himself a slaveholding Virginian. Jefferson understood the contradiction, and his draft sharply condemned the slave trade — although not slavery itself — calling it "a cruel war against human nature." But the Continental Congress, America's de facto government at the time, deleted the slave trade reference from the Declaration to avoid any controversy that might fracture its pro-independence consensus. It would not be the last time that political expediency would trump moral imperatives.

By 1787, many Americans had determined to replace the existing loose, decentralized alliance of 13 states with a stronger federal government. The Constitutional Convention, held in Philadelphia from May to September of that year, produced a blueprint for such a government. "There were big fights over slavery at the convention," according to David Stewart, author of *The Summer of 1787: The Men Who Invented the Constitution*. While "many of the delegates were actually abolitionist in their views ... there was not a feel for abolition in the country at the time."

Because any proposed constitution would not take effect until ratified by 9 of the 13 states, it became necessary to reach a compromise on the status of the African-American slaves. Northern delegates to the convention, led by James Wilson of Pennsylvania, reached an agreement with three large slaveholding states. Both sides agreed that every five "unfree persons" — slaves — would count as three people when calculating the size of a state's congressional delegation. They also agreed to bar the U.S. Congress for 20 years from passing any law prohibiting the importation of slaves. (Congress later would abolish the slave trade, effective 1808. By then, this was not a controversial measure owing to the natural increase of the slave population.)

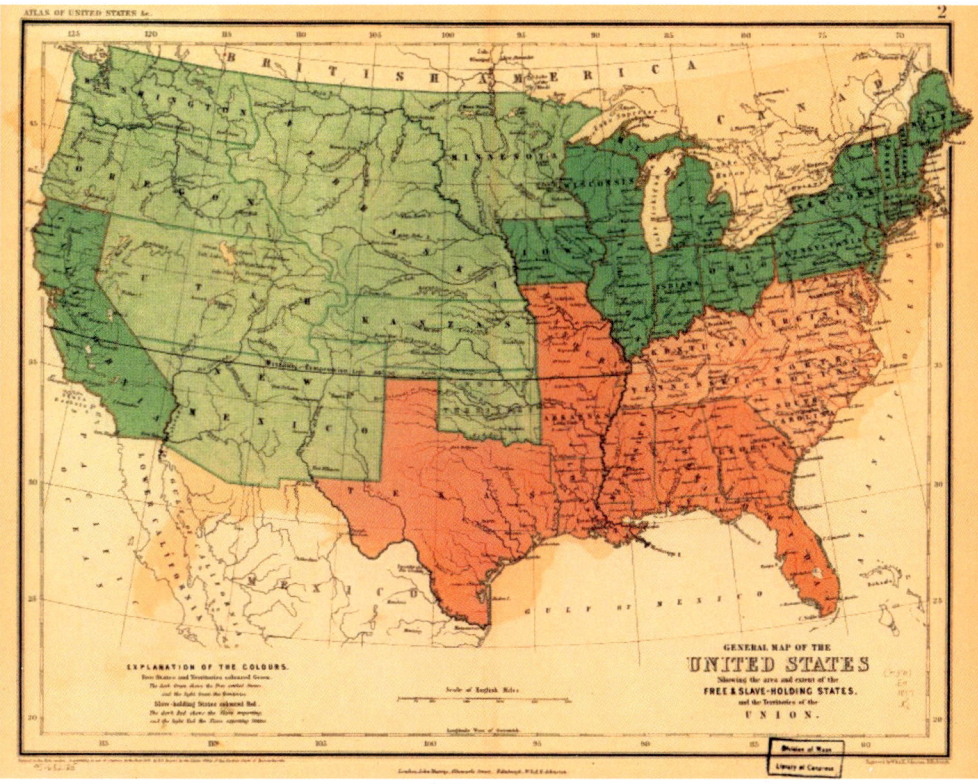

This map of the United States in 1857 depicts the "free" states in dark green, slave states in red and light red, and the territories (American lands not yet admitted to statehood) in light green.

This "three-fifths compromise" has been described as America's Faustian bargain, or original sin. As David Walker, a free northern black, argued in an 1829 pamphlet: "Has Mr. Jefferson declared to the world that we are inferior to the whites, both in the endowments of our bodies and of minds?" The compromise allowed the states to form a stronger union, but it also ensured that slavery would continue in the South, where the 1793 invention of the cotton gin had sparked the growth of a slave-intensive plantation system of cotton cultivation. It also bore profound political consequences for the young nation. In the hotly contested presidential election of 1800, the additional electoral votes awarded southern states by virtue of their slave populations supplied Thomas Jefferson with his margin of victory over the incumbent president, John Adams of Massachusetts.

Of even greater importance was how slavery affected the nation's expansion. The question of whether new states would permit slavery assumed decisive importance upon the congressional balance-of-power between the "slave" and "free" states. During the first half of the 19th century, Congress hammered out a number of compromises that generally ensured that states allowing slavery would enter the Union paired with new states that prohibited it. The Missouri Compromise, the Compromise of 1850, and the Kansas-Nebraska Act all maintained this political balance. In 1857, however, the Supreme Court ruled in the *Dred Scott v. Sanford* case that Congress could not bar slavery in western territories not yet admitted as states. The decision intensified the sectional conflict over slavery and hastened the ultimate confrontation to come.

Even as the young nation's political system failed to secure for African Americans the civil rights enjoyed by their white countrymen, brave men and women were launching efforts to abolish slavery and to ensure that the United States would live up to its own best ideals.

FREE AT LAST: THE U.S. CIVIL RIGHTS MOVEMENT 9

The Pen of Frederick Douglass

Although the U.S. political system proved unable to dislodge slavery from the American South, the "peculiar institution," as southerners often called it, did not go unchallenged. Determined women and men — blacks and whites — devoted their lives to the cause of abolition, the legal prohibition of slavery. They employed an array of tactics, both violent and nonviolent. And just as in Martin Luther King's day, the pen and the appeal to conscience would prove a powerful weapon. While the American Civil War was not solely a battle to free the slaves, the abolitionists persuaded many northerners to concur with the sentiment expressed in 1858 by a senatorial candidate named Abraham Lincoln: "A house divided against itself cannot stand. I believe this government cannot endure, permanently half slave and half free."

An anti-slavery meeting in Boston, 1835, attracts both whites and free blacks.

The stirring words of African-American and white thinkers forced increasing numbers of their countrymen to confront the contradiction between their noble ideals and the lives of bondage imposed on black Americans in the South. Perhaps the most powerful pen belonged to Frederick Douglass, an escaped slave, journalist, publisher, and champion of liberty. Douglass was born into slavery in either 1817 or 1818. His mistress defied Maryland state law by teaching the boy to read. At age 13 he purchased his first book, a collection of essays, poems, and dialogues extolling liberty that was widely used in early 19th-century American schoolrooms. From these youthful studies, Douglass began to hone the skills that would make him one of the century's most powerful and effective orators. In 1838, Douglass escaped from the plantation where he worked as a field hand and arrived in New Bedford, Massachusetts, where he would launch a remarkable career.

In 1841, the leading white abolitionist, William Lloyd Garrison, sponsored an anti-slavery convention held in Nantucket, Massachusetts. One attendee familiar with Douglass's talks at local black churches invited him to address the gathering. "It was with the utmost difficulty that I could stand erect," Douglass later wrote, "or that I could command and articulate two words without hesitation and stammering." But his words moved the crowd: "The audience sympathized with me at once, and from having been remarkably quiet, became much excited." The convention organizers agreed. Their Massachusetts Anti-Slavery Society immediately hired Douglass as an agent.

In his new career, Douglass spoke at public meetings throughout the North. He condemned slavery and argued that African Americans were entitled by right to the civil rights that the U.S. Constitution afforded other Americans. On a number of occasions, racist mobs attacked these abolitionist gatherings, but other whites befriended Douglass and championed his cause. After one mob knocked out the teeth of a white colleague who saved Douglass from violent attack, Douglass wrote his friend: "I shall never forget how like two very brothers we were ready to dare, do, and even die for each other." Douglass praised his colleague's willingness to leave a "life of ease and even luxury ... against the wishes of your father and many of your friends," instead to do "something toward breaking the fetters of the slave and elevating the dispised [sic] black man."

In 1845, Douglass published the first of several acclaimed autobiographies. His writings educated white Americans about plantation life, disabused them of the notion that slavery was somehow "good" for blacks, and convinced many that no just society could tolerate the practice. But with Douglass's sudden fame came a real danger: that his master might find and recapture him. Douglass prudently left the country for a two-year speaking tour of England, Scotland, and Ireland. While Douglass was overseas, his friends purchased his freedom — the price for one of the nation's greatest men was just over $700.

In Great Britain, Douglass was exposed to a more politically aggressive brand of abolitionism. When he returned to the United States in 1847, Douglass broke with William Lloyd Garrison. Garrison favored purely moral and nonviolent action against slavery, and he was willing to see the North secede from the Union to avoid slavery's "moral stain." Douglass pointed out that such a course would do little for black slaves in the South, and he offered his support for a range of more aggressive activities. He backed mainstream political parties promising to prevent the extension of slavery into the western territories and other parties demanding complete nationwide abolition. He offered his house as a station on the Underground Railroad (the name given to a network of people who helped fugitive slaves escape to the North) and befriended the militant abolitionist John Brown, who aimed to spark a violent slave uprising.

In 1847, Douglass launched *The North Star*, the first of several newspapers he would publish to promote the causes of equal rights for blacks and for women. Its motto was "Right is of no Sex — Truth is of no Color — God is the Father of us all, and we are all brethren." Douglass was an early and fervent champion of gender equality. In 1872, he would run for vice president on an Equal Rights Party ticket headed by Victoria Claflin Woodhull, the United States' first woman presidential candidate.

Douglass campaigned for Abraham Lincoln in the 1860 presidential election. When the American Civil War — pitting the northern Union against the rebellious southern Confederacy — broke out shortly after Lincoln's inauguration, Douglass argued that the Union should employ black troops: "Once let the black man get upon his person the brass letters, U.S.; let him get an eagle on his button, and a musket on his shoulder, and bullets in his pocket, and there is no power on earth which can deny that he has earned the right to citizenship." Too old himself to fight, Douglass recruited black soldiers for the 54th and 55th Massachusetts Regiments, two black-manned units that fought with great valor.

During the great conflict, Douglass's relations with Lincoln initially were choppy, as the president worked first to conciliate the slaveholding border states crucial to the Union war effort. On September 22, 1862, however, Lincoln issued the Emancipation Proclamation, declaring the freedom — on January 1, 1863 — of all slaves held in the areas still in rebellion. In March 1863, Lincoln endorsed the recruitment of black soldiers, and the following year he flatly rejected suggestions to enter into peace negotiations before the South agreed to abolish slavery. The president twice invited Douglass to meet with him at the White House. Douglass later wrote of Lincoln that "in his company I was never in any way reminded of my humble origin, or of my unpopular color," and the president received him "just as you have seen one gentleman receive another."

Douglass's remarkable career continued after the war's end. He worked for passage of the Thirteenth, Fourteenth, and Fifteenth Amendments to the U.S. Constitution — the postwar amendments that spelled out rights that applied to all men, not just to whites, and prohibited the individual states from denying those rights. While it would take a later generation of brave civil rights champions to ensure that these amendments would be honored, they would build on the constitutional foundation laid by Douglass and others. Douglass went on to hold a number of local offices in the capital city of Washington, D.C., and to continue his work for women's suffrage and equality. He died in 1895, by any fair reckoning the leading African-American figure of the 19th century.

The Underground Railroad

Frederick Douglass was a man of singular abilities. His contemporaries, both white and African American pursued a variety of tactics to combat slavery and win blacks their civil rights. In a nation that was half slave and half free, one obvious tactic was to spirit slaves northward to freedom. Members of several religious denominations took the lead. Beginning around 1800, a number of Quakers (a religious denomination founded in England and influential in Pennsylvania) began to offer runaway slaves refuge and assistance either to start new lives in the North or to reach Canada. "Fugitive Slave" laws enacted in 1793 and 1850 provided for the seizure and return of runaway slaves, but the Quakers were willing nonviolently to disobey what they considered unjust laws.

Harriet Tubman leading escaped slaves to freedom in Canada.

Evangelical Methodists, Presbyterians, and Congregationalists subsequently joined the effort, which expanded to help greater numbers of escaped slaves find their way out of the South.

Free blacks came to assume increasingly prominent roles in the movement, which became known as the Underground Railroad, not because it employed tunnels or trains — it used neither — but for the railroad language it employed. A "conductor" familiar with the local area would spirit one or more slaves to a "station," typically the home of a sympathizing "stationmaster," then to another station, and so on, until the slaves reached free territory. The slaves would normally travel under cover of darkness, usually about 16 to 32 kilometers per night. This was extremely dangerous work. Conductors and slaves alike faced harsh punishment or death if they were captured.

The most famous conductor was a woman, an escaped African-American slave named Harriet Tubman. After reaching freedom in 1849, Tubman returned to the South on some 20 Underground Railroad missions that rescued about 300 slaves, including Tubman's own sister, brother, and parents. She was a master of disguise, posing at times as a harmless old woman or a deranged old man. No slave in Tubman's care was ever captured. African Americans looking northward called her "Moses," and the Ohio River that divided slave states from free states in parts of the nation the "River Jordan," biblical references to reaching the Promised Land. Slaveholders offered a $40,000 reward for her capture, and John Brown called her "General Tubman."

In 1850, a sectional political compromise resulted in the passage of a new and stronger Fugitive Slave Law. While many northern states had quietly declined to enforce the previous statute, this new law established special commissioners authorized to enforce in federal court slave-masters' claims to escaped slaves. It imposed heavy penalties on federal marshals who failed to enforce its terms, and on anyone who gave assistance to an escaped slave. The Underground Railroad now was forced to adopt more aggressive tactics, including daring rescues of blacks from courtrooms and even from the custody of federal marshals.

While the numbers of agents, stationmasters, and conductors was relatively small, their efforts freed tens of thousands of slaves. Their selfless bravery helped spark an increase in northern antislavery sentiment. That response, and northern resistance to the Fugitive Slave Law of 1850, convinced many white southerners that the North would not permanently accept a half-slave nation.

By the Sword

As early as 1663, when several Gloucester County, Virginia, blacks were beheaded for plotting rebellion, African-American slaves launched a number of rebellions against their slave masters. They could look for inspiration to Haiti, where native resistance expelled the French colonizers, ended their slave-plantation labor system, and established an independent republic. In Philadelphia, Pennsylvania, a successful black entrepreneur named James Forten concluded that African Americans similarly "could not always be detained in their present bondage." In the American South, white plantation owners feared he might be right, and they reacted brutally to even the slightest tremor of possible rebellion.

Even so, some brave African Americans were determined to take up arms against impossible odds. Perhaps the best-known struggle occurred in Virginia in 1831. Nat Turner (1800-1831) was a slave in Southampton County, Virginia. His first master allowed Turner to be schooled in reading, writing, and religion. Turner began to preach, attracted followers, and, by some accounts, came to believe himself divinely appointed to lead his people to freedom. On August 22, 1831, Turner and a group of between 50 and 75 slaves armed themselves with knives, hatchets, and axes. Over two days, they moved from house to house, freeing the slaves they met and killing more than 50 white Virginians, many of them women and children.

The response was as swift as it was crushing. Local militia hunted down the rebels, 48 of whom would be tried and 18 of whom were hanged. Turner escaped, but on October 30 he was cornered in a cave. After trial and conviction, Turner was hanged and his body flayed, beheaded, and quartered. Meanwhile, mobs of vengeful whites attacked any blacks they could find, regardless of their involvement in the Turner revolt. About 200 blacks were beaten, lynched, or murdered.

The political consequences of the Nat Turner rebellion extended far beyond Southampton County. The antislavery movement was suppressed throughout the South, with harsh new laws curtailing black liberties more tightly than ever before. Meanwhile in Boston, William Lloyd Garrison tarred as hypocrites those who blamed the antislavery movement for Turner's revolt. The slaves, Garrison argued, had fought for the

A depiction of the 1831 Virginia slave rebellion led by Nat Turner.

very liberties that white Americans proudly celebrated at every turn:

> *Ye accuse the pacific friends of emancipation of instigating the slaves to revolt. Take back the charge as a foul slander. The slaves need no incentives at our hands. They will find them in their stripes — in their emaciated bodies — in their ceaseless toil — in their ignorant minds — in every field, in every valley, on every hill-top and mountain, wherever you and your fathers have fought for liberty — in your speeches, your conversations, your celebrations, your pamphlets, your newspapers — voices in the air, sounds from across the ocean, invitations to resistance above, below, around them! What more do they need? Surrounded by such influences, and smarting under their newly made wounds, is it wonderful [surprising] that they should rise to contend — as other "heroes" have contended — for their lost rights? It is not wonderful.*

The Rebellious John Brown

John Brown, pictured here circa 1859, led an ill-fated raid on Harpers Ferry, West Virginia (then Virginia), in hopes of sparking a wider slave rebellion.

Another famous effort to free the African-American slaves by the sword was led by a white American. John Brown, a native New Englander, had long mulled the idea of achieving abolition by force and had, in 1847, confided to Frederick Douglass his intent to do precisely that. In 1855, Brown arrived in the Kansas Territory, scene of violent clashes between pro- and antislavery factions. At issue was whether Kansas would be admitted to the Union as a "free-soil" or slave state. Each faction built its own settlements.

After slavery advocates conducted a raid on "free" Lawrence, Kansas, Brown and four of his sons, on May 24, 1856, carried out the Pottawatomie Massacre, descending on the slaveholding village of Pottawatomie and killing five men. Brown then launched a series of guerrilla actions against armed pro-slavery bands. He returned to New England, hoping — unsuccessfully — to raise an African-American fighting force and — more successfully — to raise funds from leading abolitionists.

After a convention of Brown supporters meeting in Canada declared him commander-in-chief of a provisional government to depose southern slaveholders, Brown established a secret base in Maryland, near Harpers Ferry, Virginia (now West Virginia). He waited there for supporters, most of whom failed to arrive. On October 16, 1859, Brown led a biracial force of about 20 that captured the federal arsenal at Harpers Ferry and held about 60 local notables hostage. The plan was to arm groups of escaped slaves and head south, liberating additional slaves as they marched. But Brown delayed too long and soon was surrounded by a company of U.S. Marines led by Lieutenant Colonel Robert E. Lee (future commander of the southern forces during the Civil War). Brown refused to surrender. Wounded and captured in the ensuing battle, Brown was tried in Virginia and convicted of treason, conspiracy, and murder.

Addressing the jury after the verdict was announced, Brown said:

> *I believe that to have interfered as I have done, as I have always freely admitted I have done in behalf of His despised poor, was not wrong, but right. Now, if it is deemed necessary that I should forfeit my life for the furtherance of the ends of justice, and mingle my blood further with the blood of my children and with the blood of millions in this slave country whose rights are disregarded by wicked, cruel, and unjust enactments, I submit; so let it be done!*

Brown was hanged on December 2, 1859, a martyr to the antislavery cause. In the Civil War that began a year later, Union soldiers marched to variants of a tune they called "John Brown's Body" (one version, penned by Julia Ward Howe, would become "The Battle Hymn of the Republic"). A typical stanza read:

> *Old John Brown's body is a-mouldering in the dust,*
>
> *Old John Brown's rifle is red with blood-spots turned to rust,*
>
> *Old John Brown's pike has made its last, unflinching thrust,*
>
> *His soul is marching on!*

Harper's Ferry, Virginia (now West Virginia), site of John Brown's infamous raid.

Abraham Lincoln depicted against the text of his Emancipation Proclamation, which freed all slaves in the still rebellious territories, effective January 1, 1863.

The American Civil War

The issue of slavery and the status of black Americans eroded relations between North and South from the first days of American independence until the election of Abraham Lincoln to the presidency in 1860. Lincoln opposed slavery, calling it a "monstrous injustice," but his primary concern was to maintain the Union. He thus was willing to accept slavery in those states where it already existed while prohibiting its further extension in the western territories. But white southerners considered Lincoln's election a threat to their social order. Beginning with South Carolina in December 1860, 11 southern states seceded from the Union, forming the Confederate States of America.

For Lincoln and for millions of northerners, the Union was, as the historian James M. McPherson has written, "a bond among all of the American people, not a voluntary association of states that could be disbanded by action of any one or several of them." As the president explained to his private secretary: "We must settle this question now, whether in a free government the minority have the right to break up the government whenever they choose." Thus, as Lincoln made clear early in the war: "My paramount object in this struggle is to save the Union, and is not either to save or to destroy slavery. If I could save the Union without freeing any slave I would do it; and if I could save it by freeing all the slaves I would do it; and if I could save it by freeing some and leaving others alone I would also do that."

But slavery drove the sectional conflict. As the brutal war wore on, many northerners grew more unwilling to abide slavery under any circumstances. Northern troops who came into firsthand contact with southern blacks often became more sympathetic to their plight. Lincoln also saw that freeing those slaves would strike at the Confederacy's economic base and hence its ability to wage war. And once freed, the former slaves could take up arms for the Union cause, thus "earning" their freedom. For all these reasons, freeing the black slaves joined preserving the Union as a northern war aim.

Lincoln's Emancipation Proclamation, effective January 1, 1863, declared all slaves in the rebellious states "thenceforward, and forever free." As he signed the document, Lincoln remarked that "I never, in my life, felt more certain that I was doing right, than I do in signing this paper."

The future African-American leader Booker T. Washington was about seven years old when the Emancipation Proclamation was read on his plantation. As he recalled in his 1901 memoir *Up From Slavery*:

As the great day drew nearer, there was more singing in the slave quarters than usual. It was bolder, had more ring, and lasted later into the night. Most of the verses of the plantation songs had some reference to freedom. ... Some man who seemed to be a stranger (a U.S. officer, I presume) made a little speech and then read a rather long paper — the Emancipation Proclamation, I think. After the reading we were told that we were all free, and could go when and where we pleased. My mother, who was standing by my side, leaned over and kissed her children, while tears of joy ran down her cheeks. She explained to us what it all meant, that this was the day for which she had been so long praying, but fearing that she would never live to see.

As a condition of regaining their congressional representation, the seceding states were obliged to ratify the Thirteenth, Fourteenth, and Fifteenth Amendments to the U.S. Constitution. These "Reconstruction Amendments" abolished slavery, guaranteed equal protection of the law — including by the states — to all citizens, and barred voting discrimination on the basis of "race, color, or previous condition of servitude." The years following the Civil War thus established the legal basis for guaranteeing African Americans the civil rights accorded other Americans. Shamefully, the plain meaning of these laws would be ignored for nearly another century, as the politics of sectional compromise again would trump justice for African Americans.

BLACK SOLDIERS IN THE CIVIL WAR

When the American Civil War began in 1861, Jacob Dodson, a free black man living in Washington, D.C., wrote to Secretary of War Simon Cameron informing him that he knew of "300 reliable colored free citizens" who wanted to enlist and defend the city. Cameron replied that "this department has no intention at present to call into the service of the government any colored soldiers." It didn't matter that black men, slave and free, had served in colonial militias and had fought on both sides of the Revolutionary War. Many black men felt that serving in the military was a way they might gain freedom and full citizenship.

Why did many military and civilian leaders reject the idea of recruiting black soldiers? Some said that black troops would prove too cowardly to fight white men, others said that they would be inferior fighters, and some thought that white soldiers would not serve with black soldiers. There were a few military leaders, though, who had different ideas.

On March 31, 1862, almost a year after the first shots of the Civil War were fired at Fort Sumter, South Carolina, Union (northern) troops commanded by General David Hunter took control of the islands off the coasts of northern Florida, Georgia, and South Carolina. Local whites who owned the rich cotton and rice plantations fled to the Confederate-controlled (southern) mainland. Most of their slaves remained on the islands, and they soon were joined by black escapees from the mainland who believed they would be liberated if only they could reach the Union lines. It would not be that simple.

Even as Hunter needed more soldiers to control the region's many tidal rivers and islands against stubborn Confederate guerrilla resistance, he observed how escaping mainland slaves were swelling the islands' black population. Perhaps, he reasoned, the African Americans could solve his manpower shortage. He devised a radical plan.

Hunter, a staunch abolitionist, took it upon himself to free the slaves — not just on the islands but through-out Confederate-controlled South Carolina, Georgia, and Florida — and to recruit black men capable of bearing arms as Union soldiers. He would attempt to train and form the first all-black regiment of the Civil War.

News traveled slowly in those days, and President Abraham Lincoln did not hear about Hunter's regiment until June. While Lincoln opposed slavery, he feared moving more quickly than public opinion in the embattled North — and particularly in the slaveholding border states that had sided with the Union — would allow. He also was adamant that "no commanding general shall do such a thing, upon my responsibility, without consulting me." In an angry

Frederick Douglass: "Once let the black man get upon his person the brass letters U.S.

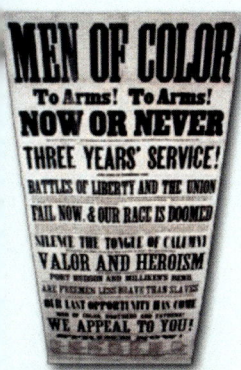

With the Emancipation Proclamation, the Union (Northern) Army began actively to recruit African-American soldiers.

letter, the president informed the general that neither he nor any other subordinate had the right to free anyone, although he carefully asserted for himself the right to emancipate slaves at a time of his choosing. Hunter was ordered to disband the regiment, but the seed he planted soon sprouted.

In August 1862, two weeks after Hunter had dismantled his regiment, the War Department allowed General Rufus Saxton to raise the Union Army's first official black regiment, the First South Carolina Volunteers. This and other black regiments organized in the coastal regions successfully defended and held the coastal islands for the duration of the war.

The First Kansas Colored Volunteers was also organized around this time, but without official War Department sanction. Meanwhile, President Lincoln had carefully laid the groundwork for emancipation and the inclusion of men of African descent into the military. As white northerners increasingly understood that black slaves were crucial to the Confederacy's economy and to its war effort, Lincoln could justify freeing the slaves as matter of military necessity.

When Abraham Lincoln signed the Emancipation Proclamation on January 1, 1863, the military's policy toward enslaved people became clearer. Those who reached the Union lines would be free. Also, the War Department began to recruit and enlist black troops for newly formed regiments of the Union Army — the United States Colored Troops (USCT). All of the officers in these regiments, however, would be white.

By the fall of 1864, some 140 black regiments had been raised in many northern states and in southern territories captured by the Union. About 180,000 African Americans served during the Civil War, including more than 75,000 northern black volunteers.

Although the black regiments were segregated from their white counterparts, they fought the same battles. Black troops performed bravely and successfully even though they coped with both the Confederate enemy and the suspicion of some of their Union military colleagues.

Once black men were accepted into the military, they were limited in many cases to garrison and fatigue duty. The famed Massachusetts 54th Regiment's Colonel Robert Gould Shaw actively petitioned superiors to give his men a chance to engage in battle and prove themselves as soldiers. Some of the other officers who knew what their men could do did the same. Black troops had to fight to get the same pay as white soldiers. Some regiments refused to accept lower pay. It was not until 1865, the year the war ended, that Congress passed a law providing equal pay for black soldiers.

Despite these restrictions, the United States Colored Troops successfully participated in 449 military engagements, 39 of them major battles. They fought in battles in South Carolina, Louisiana, Florida, Virginia, Tennessee, Alabama, and other states. They bravely stormed forts and faced artillery knowing that if captured by the enemy, they would not be given the rights of prisoners of war, but instead would be sold into slavery. The black troops performed with honor and valor all of the duties of soldiers.

Despite the Army's policy of only having white officers, eventually about 100 black soldiers rose from the ranks and were commissioned as officers. Eight black surgeons also received commissions in the USCT. More than a dozen USCT soldiers were given the Congressional Medal of Honor for bravery.

In 1948, President Harry S. Truman ordered the desegregation of the armed forces. Today's military remains an engine of social and economic opportunity for black Americans. But it was the sacrifices of the Civil War-era black soldiers that paved the way for the full acceptance of African Americans in the United States military. More fundamentally, their efforts were an important part of the struggle of African Americans for liberty and dignity.

By Joyce Hansen
A four-time winner of the Coretta Scott King Honor Book Award, Joyce Hansen has published short stories and 15 books of contemporary and historical fiction and non-fiction for young readers, including *Between Two Fires: Black Soldiers in the Civil War*.

3

"Separate but Equal"

AFRICAN AMERICANS RESPOND TO THE FAILURE OF RECONSTRUCTION

This reconstruction-era wood engraving depicts a Freedman's Bureau representative standing between armed white and black Americans. The failure of Reconstruction would usher in the era of "Jim Crow" segregation in the American South.

More than 600,000 Americans perished in the Civil War. Their sacrifice resolved some of the nation's most intractable conflicts. Slavery at last was prohibited, and the principle that no state could secede from the Union was established. But incompatible visions of American society persisted, and the consequences for African Americans would prove immense.

One vision, associated during the 19th and early 20th centuries with the Democratic Party, blended American individualism and suspicion of big government with a preference for local and state authority over federal power, and, at least in the South, a dogged belief in white superiority. The Republican Party, founded in the 1850s, was more willing to employ federal power to promote economic development. Its core belief was often called "free labor." For millions of northerners, free labor meant that a man — the concept then generally applied only to men — could work where and how he wanted, could accumulate property in his own name, and, most importantly, was free to rise as far as his talents and abilities might take him.

Abraham Lincoln was a model of this self-made man. As president, he would boast: "I am not ashamed to confess that 25 years ago I was a hired laborer, mauling rails, at work on a flat-boat. ... " Even as many Republicans condemned slavery as immoral, all viewed the South as lagging in both economic growth and social mobility. As the historian Antonia Etheart has written, Republicans saw in the South "an unchangeable

18 FREE AT LAST: THE U.S. CIVIL RIGHTS MOVEMENT

hierarchy dominated by the aristocracy of slaveholders."

After the North's military victory ended slavery, its free-labor ideology required that the freedmen possess their civil rights. During the years that followed the Civil War, northern Republicans at first were determined to "reconstruct" the South along free-labor principles. Although many white southerners resisted, northern military might for a time ensured blacks the right to vote, to receive an education, and, generally, to enjoy the constitutional privileges afforded other Americans. But northerners' determination to support blacks' aspirations gradually ebbed as their desire for reconciliation with the South deepened. By the end of the 19th century, southern elites had reversed many black gains and imposed an oppressive system of legal segregation.

Congressional Reconstruction

The assassination of Abraham Lincoln in April 1865 elevated Vice President Andrew Johnson to the presidency. Johnson, a Tennessee Democrat chosen as Lincoln's 1864 running mate to signal moderation and a desire for postwar reconciliation, moved swiftly to readmit the former Confederate states to full membership in the Union. Southern states were obliged to ratify the Thirteenth Amendment, prohibiting slavery. But they were not required to protect the equality and civil rights of their African-American populations. White-dominated southern state governments organized under Johnson's guidelines swiftly adopted Black Codes — punitive statutes that closely regulated the behavior of supposedly "free" African Americans. These laws typically imposed curfews, banned possession of firearms, and even imprisoned as vagrants former slaves who left their plantations without permission. Meanwhile, Johnson ordered the restoration of abandoned southern plantations to their former slave-master owners.

Many northerners were outraged. Surely, they argued, they had not fought and died only to re-empower the racist southern aristocracy. The 1866 congressional election returned large numbers of "Radical Republicans" determined to ensure greater civil rights for blacks, and, more generally, through government power to reconstruct the South along northern lines. This 40th Congress refused to seat members elected under Johnson-authorized southern state governments. It then overrode Johnson's veto to enact several important civil rights laws.

One such law extended the operations of the Freedman's Bureau. Established before Lincoln's death, this federal agency helped ease the freed slaves' transition to freedom. It supplied medical care, built hundreds of schools to educate black children, and helped freed slaves negotiate labor contracts with their former owners and other employers.

A second law, the Civil Rights Act of 1866, declared that all persons born in the United States were citizens, without regard to race, color, or previous condition. African Americans thus were entitled to make and enforce contracts, sue and be sued, and own property.

Because Johnson opposed and arguably attempted to subvert the application of these and other measures, the House of Representatives in 1868 impeached (indicted) Johnson, thus initiating the constitutionally proscribed method for removing a president from office. The Senate acquitted Johnson by one vote, but for the remainder of his term, he mostly refrained from challenging Congress's reconstruction program.

Most important of all, Congress made clear that the formerly rebellious states would not be permitted to regain their congressional representation until they ratified the proposed Fourteenth Amendment to the U.S. Constitution. This amendment would supply the legal bedrock on which the modern civil rights movement would stake its claim for racial equality. The first 10 amendments, known collectively as the Bill of Rights, had protected Americans against encroachments by the federal government. This afforded African Americans little or no protection against racist laws enacted by state governments. The Fourteenth Amendment, ratified in July 1868, remedied this. "No State," it reads, shall "deprive any person of life, liberty, or property, without due process of law; nor deny to any person within its jurisdiction the equal protection of the laws." The Fifteenth Amendment,

The assassination of Abraham Lincoln brought the southerner Andrew Johnson to the presidency. Here, Johnson pardons white rebels for taking up arms against the Union.

adopted shortly afterward, declared that the "right of citizens of the United States to vote shall not be denied or abridged by the United States or by any state on account of race, color, or previous condition of servitude."

Temporary Gains ... and Reverses

With northern troops enforcing Reconstruction legislation throughout much of the South, African Americans scored major gains. The apparatus of the slave system — slave quarters, gang labor, and the like — was dismantled. Blacks increasingly founded their own churches. Headed by black ministers, these would provide the organizational sinew on which Martin Luther King Jr. and others later would build the modern civil rights movement.

Black voters aligned with a small faction of southern whites to elect Republican-led governments in several southern states. Many blacks held important public offices at the state and county levels. Two African Americans were elected to the U.S. Senate, and 14 to the House of Representatives. Typical was Benjamin Sterling Turner, Alabama's first black congressman. Born into slavery, Turner was freed by Lincoln's Emancipation Proclamation. He swiftly established himself as an entrepreneur and then was elected tax collector and city councilman in Selma, the site of a crucial 20th-century civil rights struggle. Elected to Congress in 1870, Turner secured monthly pensions for black Civil War veterans and fought for greater federal expenditures in his district.

Republican-led state governments in the Reconstruction-era South typically raised taxes and expanded social services. Among their innovations were state-supported educational systems and measures to subsidize economic growth. African Americans were major beneficiaries of these innovations, and for a time it seemed as if their civil rights might be permanently secured.

But the majority of southern whites were determined to resist black equality. Many could not unlearn the harsh stereotypes of black inferiority on which they had been raised. Many southern whites were very poor, and they grounded their identity in a perceived sense of racial superiority. Southern elites understood that this racial divide could block interracial political efforts to advance their common economic interests. They often employed white racial resentment as a tool to regain political power.

White southerners, associated in this era with the Democratic Party, launched a blistering political attack on white southern Republicans. They called the native southerners "scalawags," a term derived from a word meaning "undersized or worthless animal"; the northerners who sought their fortune in the postwar South were called "carpetbaggers" because these newcomers allegedly carried their belongings in travel bags made of carpet.

The reaction against newly empowered African Americans was harsher still. Secret terrorist organizations such as the Knights of the White Camellia — named for the snow-white bloom of a southern flowering shrub and intended to symbolize the purity of the white race — and the Ku Klux Klan (KKK) launched violent attacks to intimidate black voters and keep them away from the polls. President Ulysses S. Grant dispatched three regiments of infantry and a flotilla of gunboats to ensure fair elections in New Orleans in 1874. Grant used federal troops to smash the Klan, but the violence continued as militant whites formed informal "social clubs" described by historian James M. McPherson as "paramilitary organizations that functioned as armed auxiliaries of the Democratic Party in southern states in their drive to 'redeem' the South from 'black and tan Negro-Carpetbag rule.'"

Some northern whites feared that Grant had gone too far, and more simply wearied of the struggle. As McPherson writes:

> Many Northerners adopted a "plague on both your houses" attitude toward the White Leagues and the "Negro-Carpetbag" state governments. Withdraw the federal troops, they said, and let the southern people work out their own problems even if that meant a solid South for the white-supremacy Democratic Party.

This was essentially what happened. In elections marred

U.S. Representative Benjamin Sterling Turner was elected to Congress from Reconstruction-era Alabama. With the end of Reconstruction and the withdrawal of Union troops from the South, black Americans in that region were systematically deprived of their political rights.

by fraud, intimidation, and violence, Democrats gradually regained control of state governments throughout the South. In 1877, a political bargain declared Republican Rutherford B. Hayes the winner of the closely contested 1876 presidential election. In exchange, Hayes withdrew the last federal troops from the South. Black Americans, the overwhelming majority of whom then lived in the states of the former Confederacy, were again at the mercy of racist state laws.

The Advent of "Jim Crow"

During the years that followed, and especially after 1890, state governments in the South adopted segregationist laws mandating separation of the races in nearly every aspect of everyday life. They required separate public schools, railroad cars, and public libraries; separate water fountains, restaurants, and hotels. The system became known informally as "Jim Crow," from the 1828 minstrel show song "Jump Jim Crow," which was typically performed by white performers in blackface as a caricature of the unlettered, inferior black man.

Jim Crow could not have existed had the federal courts interpreted broadly the relevant constitutional protections. But the judicial branch instead seized upon technicalities and loopholes to avoid striking down segregationist laws. In 1875, Congress enacted what would be the last civil rights law for nearly a century. The Civil Rights Act of 1875 barred "any person" from depriving citizens of any race or color of equal treatment in public accommodations such as inns, theaters, and places of public amusement, and in public transportation. In 1883, the Supreme Court declared the law unconstitutional, reasoning that the Fourteenth Amendment prohibited discrimination by states but not by individuals. Congress accordingly could not prohibit individual acts of discrimination.

Perhaps the most significant judicial decision came in 1896. Six years earlier, Louisiana had adopted a law requiring separate rail cars for whites, blacks, and "coloreds" of mixed ancestry. An interracial group of citizens who opposed the law persuaded Homer Plessy, a public education advocate with a white complexion and a black great-grandmother, to test the law. Plessy purchased a ticket for a "whites-only" rail car. After taking his seat, Plessy revealed his ancestry to the train conductor. He was arrested, and the litigation began.

In 1896, the case reached the U.S. Supreme Court. In a seven-to-one decision, the court upheld the Louisiana law. "The enforced separation of the two races," did not, the majority ruled, "stamp the colored race with a badge of inferiority." If black Americans disagreed, that was their own interpretation and not that of the statute. Thus did the high court lend its prestige and its imprimatur to what became known as "separate but equal" segregation.

One problem with *Plessy* (formally, *Plessy v. Ferguson*), as later civil rights advocates tirelessly would document, was that separate never really was equal. Public schools and other facilities designated colored nearly always were inferior. Often they were shockingly so. But more fundamentally, the issue was whether a fair reading of the Constitution might justify separating Americans on the basis of race. As John Marshall Harlan, the dissenting justice in the *Plessy* case, argued in words that resonate to this day:

> In view of the Constitution, in the eye of the law, there is in this country no superior, dominant, ruling class of citizens. There is no caste here. Our Constitution is color-blind, and neither knows nor tolerates classes among citizens. In respect of civil rights, all citizens are equal before the law.

Justice Harlan's view would at last prevail in 1954, when the Supreme Court's unanimous *Brown v. Board of Education* decision overruled *Plessy*. For African Americans, however, the rise of Jim Crow segregation required new responses, new strategies for claiming their civil rights.

Booker T. Washington: The Quest for Economic Independence

The failure of Reconstruction and the rise of legal segregation forced African Americans to make difficult choices. The overwhelming majority still lived in the South and faced fierce, even violent resistance to civil equality. Some concluded that direct political efforts to assert their civil rights would be futile. Led by Booker T. Washington (1856-1915), they

Booker T. Washington championed economic empowerment as the means of achieving future African-American political gains.

argued instead for focusing on black economic development. Others, including most prominently the leading scholar and intellectual William Edward Burghardt (W.E.B.) Du Bois, insisted upon an uncompromising effort to achieve the voting and other civil rights promised by the Constitution and its postwar amendments.

Born into slavery, Booker T. Washington was about nine years old at the time of emancipation. He attended Hampton Normal and Agricultural Institute — today's Hampton University — in southeastern Virginia, excelled at his studies, and found work as a schoolteacher. In 1881 he was offered the opportunity to head a new school for African Americans in Macon County, Alabama.

Washington had concluded that practical skills and economic independence were the keys to black advancement. He decided to ground his new school, renamed the Tuskegee Normal and Industrial Institute (now Tuskegee University) in industrial education. Male students learned skills such as carpentry and blacksmithing, females typically studied nursing or dressmaking. Tuskegee also trained schoolteachers to staff African-American schools throughout the South. This approach promised to develop economically productive black citizens without forcing the nation to confront squarely the civil rights question. A number of leading philanthropists, such as the oil magnate John D. Rockefeller, steel producer Andrew Carnegie, and Sears, Roebuck head Julius Rosenwald, all raised funds for Tuskegee. The school grew in size, reputation, and prestige.

In September 1895, Washington delivered to a predominantly white audience his famous Atlanta Compromise speech. He argued that the greatest danger facing African Americans

> is that in the great leap from slavery to freedom we may overlook the fact that the masses of us are to live by the productions of our hands, and fail to keep in mind that we shall prosper in proportion as we learn to dignify and glorify common labor, and put brains and skill into the common occupations of life.... It is at the bottom of life we must begin, and not at the top. Nor should we permit our grievances to overshadow our opportunities.

Not surprisingly, many whites found soothing a vision in which blacks concentrated on acquiring real estate or industrial skill rather than political office, a vision that seemingly accepted the Jim Crow system. As Washington put it in his Atlanta address: "The opportunity to earn a dollar in a factory just now is worth more than the opportunity to spend a dollar in an opera-house."

But close study of Washington's speech suggests that he did not mean to accept permanent inequality. Instead, he called for African Americans gradually to amass social capital — jobs "just now" were more valuable than the right to attend the opera. Or, as he put it more bluntly: "No race that has anything to contribute to the markets of the world is long in any degree ostracized."

Washington was the nation's leading African-American figure for many years, although increasing numbers of blacks gradually turned away from his vision. One problem was that the postwar South was itself a poor region, lagging behind the North in modernization and economic development. Opportunity for southerners, black or white, simply was not as great as Booker T. Washington hoped. His gradualist posture was also unacceptable to blacks unwilling to defer to some unspecified future date their claims for full and equal civil rights.

W.E.B. Du Bois: The Push for Political Agitation

Many blacks turned for leadership to the historian and social scientist W.E.B. Du Bois (1868-1963). A graduate of Fisk University, a historically black institution in Nashville, Tennessee, Du Bois earned a PhD in history from Harvard University and took up a professorship at Atlanta University, a school founded with the assistance of the Freedman's Bureau and specializing in the training of black teachers, librarians, and other professionals. Du Bois authored and edited a number of scholarly studies depicting black life in America. Social science, he believed, would provide the key to improving race relations.

W.E.B. Du Bois, one of the United States' leading 20th century figures, testifies before Congress in 1945.

But as legal segregation — often enforced by lynchings (extralegal and often mob-instigated seizures and killings of "criminal suspects," without trial and usually on the flimsiest of evidence) — took hold throughout the South, Du Bois gradually concluded that only direct political agitation and protest could advance African-American civil rights. Inevitably Du Bois came into dispute with Booker T. Washington, who quietly built political ties to national Republicans to secure a measure of political patronage even as his priority for American blacks remained economic development.

In 1903, Du Bois published *The Souls of Black Folk*. Described by the scholar Shelby Steele as an "impassioned reaction against a black racial ideology of accommodation and humility," *Black Folk* declared squarely that "the problem of the twentieth century is the problem of the color-line." Addressing Booker T. Washington, Du Bois argued that

> *his doctrine has tended to make the whites, North and South, shift the burden of the Negro problem to the Negro's shoulders and stand aside as critical and rather pessimistic spectators; when in fact the burden belongs to the nation, and the hands of none of us are clean if we bend not our energies to righting these great wrongs.*

Du Bois also disagreed with Washington's exclusive emphasis on artisan skills. "The Negro race, like all races," he argued in a 1903 article, "is going to be saved by its exceptional men." This "talented tenth" of African Americans "must be made leaders of thought and missionaries of culture among their people." For this task, the practical training Booker T. Washington offered at Tuskegee Institute would not suffice:

> *If we make money the object of man-training, we shall develop money-makers but not necessarily men; if we make technical skill the object of education, we may possess artisans but not, in nature, men. Men we shall have only as we make manhood the object of the work of the schools — intelligence, broad sympathy, knowledge of the world that was and is, and of the relation of men to it. ... On this foundation we may build bread winning, skill of hand, and quickness of brain, with never a fear lest the child and man mistake the means of living for the object of life.*

Two years later, Du Bois and a number of leading black intellectuals formed the Niagara Movement, a civil rights organization squarely opposed to Washington's policies of accommodation and gradualism. "We want full manhood suffrage and we want it now!" Du Bois declared. (Du Bois also advocated woman suffrage.) The Niagara group held a notable 1906 conference at Harpers Ferry, West Virginia, site of John Brown's rebellion; lobbied against Jim Crow laws; distributed pamphlets and circulars; and attempted generally to raise the issues of civil rights and racial justice. But the movement was weakly organized and poorly funded. It disbanded in 1910. A new and stronger organization was ready to take its place by then.

A false charge that a black man had attempted to rape a white woman led to anti-black rioting in Springfield, Illinois, in August 1908. The riots left seven dead and forced thousands of African Americans to flee the city. The suffragette Mary White Ovington led a call for an organizational meeting of reformers. "The spirit of the abolitionists must be revived," she later wrote. Her group soon expanded and linked up with Du Bois and other African-American activists. In 1910, they founded the National Association for the Advancement of Colored People (NAACP). The new organization's leadership included white Americans, many of them Jewish, and Du Bois, who assumed the editorship of the NAACP's influential magazine *The Crisis*.

Beginning in 1913, when President Woodrow Wilson, a native southerner, permitted the segregation of the federal civil service, the NAACP turned to the courts, initiating the decades-long legal effort to overturn Jim Crow. Under Du Bois's leadership, *The Crisis* analyzed current affairs and featured the works of the great writers of the Harlem Renaissance of the 1920s and 1930s, among them Langston Hughes and Countee Cullen. By some estimates, its circulation exceeded 100,000.

Du Bois continued to write, cementing a reputation as one of the century's major American thinkers. He emerged as a leading anticolonialist and expert on African history. In 1934, Du Bois broke with the integrationist NAACP over his advocacy of Pan-African nationalism and the growing Marxist and socialist aspects of his thought. Du Bois would live on into his 90s, dying a Ghanaian citizen and committed Communist.

But the NAACP, the organization he helped to found, would launch the modern civil rights struggle.

MARCUS GARVEY:
ANOTHER PATH

Marcus Garvey (1887-1940), a major black nationalist of the early 20th century, was born in Jamaica but spent his most successful years in the United States. An enthusiastic capitalist, he believed that African Americans and other black persons around the world should make a united effort to form institutions that could concentrate wealth and power in their own hands. To this end he formed, among other organizations, the United Negro Improvement Association (UNIA). After reading Booker T. Washington's *Up From Slavery*, Garvey asked himself: "Where is the black man's government? Where is his king and kingdom? Where is his president, his country, his ambassadors, his army, his navy, and his men of big affairs? I could not find them. I decided, I will help to make them."

Garvey was born in the parish of St. Ann, Jamaica, where in his early teens he was apprenticed to his godfather, a printer named Alfred Burrowes. Garvey's father was a bookish man, as was Burrowes, and the youthful Marcus received early exposure to the world of letters. Migrating to Kingston, Garvey displayed highly refined talents as a typesetter and developed an interest in journalism.

After being blacklisted for attempting to organize workers, he left Jamaica to visit Latin America, and he later spent two years in England. During these years, he studied informally at the University of London and worked for the Sudanese-Egyptian black nationalist, Duse Mohammed Ali, founder of *The African Times* and *Orient Review*.

Garvey was determined to spread his program of black empowerment in the United States. Arriving in 1915, Garvey argued that African Americans could command respect by building their economic power. To that end, he strove to establish a network of black-owned businesses: grocery stores, laundries, and others capable of thriving independently of the white economy. While these and other initial attempts to organize the masses met with little success, Garvey's perseverance earned him increasing fame; by the end of the First World War, his name was widely known among black Americans.

Garvey was a master at manipulating the media and at staging dramatic public events. He founded his own newspaper, *Negro World*, which was distributed widely throughout the United States and in some Latin American countries. He held colorful annual conventions in New York City, where men and women marched under a banner of red, black, and green. This flag, along with other tricolored emblems, remains popular among African Americans to the present day. The striking military regalia sometimes worn by Garveyites demonstrated the nationalistic and militaristic

The black nationalist Marcus Garvey represented one strand of African-American thought. Most blacks, however, would choose to fight for equality and full participation in U.S. political and economic life.

24 FREE AT LAST: THE U.S. CIVIL RIGHTS MOVEMENT

BIG MASS MEETING
A CALL TO THE
COLORED CITIZENS
OF
ATLANTA, GEORGIA
To Hear the Great West Indian Negro Leader
HON. MARCUS GARVEY
President of the Universal Negro Improvement Association
of Jamaica, West Indies.

Big Bethel A. M. E. Church
Corner Auburn Avenue and Butler Street

SUNDAY AFTERNOON, AT 3 O'CLOCK
MARCH 25, 1917

He brings a message of inspiration to the 12,000,000 of our people in this country.

SUBJECT:
"The Negroes of the West Indies, after 78 years of Emancipation." With a general talk on the world position of the race.

An orator of exceptional force, Professor Garvey has spoken to packed audiences in England, New York, Boston, Washington, Philadelphia, Chicago, Milwaukee, St. Louis, Detroit, Cleveland, Cincinnati, Indianapolis, Louisville, Nashville and other cities. He has travelled to the principal countries of Europe, and was the first Negro to speak to the Veterans' Club of London, England.
This is the only chance to hear a great man who has taken his message before the world. COME OUT EARLY TO SECURE SEATS. It is worth travelling 1,000 miles to hear.

All Invited. Rev. R. H. Singleton, D.D., Pastor.

Advertisement for a 1917 Marcus Garvey speech.

image that his black nationalist movement strove to convey.

There is a legend that once a Congolese leader in a remote African village was asked if he knew anything about the United States. His response was said to be, "I know the name of Marcus Garvey."

Under the name of the Black Star Line, the UNIA launched an abortive attempt to open up the world to black-owned commerce. The organization sold impressive amounts of stock in this enterprise, mostly in small amounts to ordinary working people, and purchased several steamships, unfortunately in dilapidated condition.

Garvey believed in separation of the races and was willing to cooperate with leaders of white racist organizations, notably the Ku Klux Klan. After meeting with Klan leadership, he came under attack from several already-hostile black leaders. A. Philip Randolph, founder and leader of the Brotherhood of Sleeping Car Porters, America's earliest successful, predominantly black labor union, was particularly hostile.

Randolph accused Garvey of cooperating with white racists in a scheme to repatriate American blacks back to Africa. Garvey denied any such ambitions, but he did send emissaries to the Republic of Liberia to investigate the prospects of new business undertakings, and he found considerable sympathy for his ideas among young African intellectuals.

In 1925, Garvey was imprisoned on federal charges of using the mails to defraud. He denied the charge, and even some of his critics found it unfair. President Calvin Coolidge pardoned Garvey in 1927, but as a convicted felon who was not a U.S. citizen, Garvey was immediately deported to his native Jamaica. W.E.B. Du Bois, one of Garvey's severest critics, wished him well, encouraging him to pursue his efforts in his own country.

Establishing himself in London, England, Garvey launched a new magazine, *The Black Man*, which criticized such prominent black American figures as the heavyweight boxing champion Joe Louis, the entertainer and political activist Paul Robeson, and the controversial spiritual figure Father Divine for their failure to supply effective race leadership. But Garvey was unable there either to rebuild his organization to its previous membership levels. He retained sufficient U.S. popularity to draw an attentive audience to a meeting in Windsor, Ontario, just across the river from Detroit, Michigan, a base for Garvey's earlier activism. His final operations were conducted from London, England, where he died in 1940.

By **Wilson Jeremiah Moses**
Moses is Ferree Professor of History at the Pennsylvania State University and author of the scholarly article "Marcus Garvey: A Reappraisal." His books include *The Golden Age of Black Nationalism, 1850-1925*.

4

CHARLES HAMILTON HOUSTON AND THURGOOD MARSHALL
LAUNCH THE LEGAL CHALLENGE TO SEGREGATION

In November 1956, a black-instigated boycott of the segregated bus system in Montgomery, Alabama, had entered its 12th month. A year earlier, a black woman named Rosa Parks had bravely refused to relinquish her front seat on a municipal bus to a white man, launching a political movement and introducing Americans to a courageous and dynamic leader — the Reverend Dr. Martin Luther King Jr. But it was not until the courts forbade the relegation of African Americans to the back of the bus that the city of Montgomery yielded and the boycott succeeded. As historian Kevin Mumford has written: "Without constitutional legitimacy and the promise of protection from the courts, local black protesters would be crushed by state and local officials, and white segregationists could easily prevail."

Americans often refer to the mid-20th-century social justice campaigns led by King and others as the civil rights movement. As we have seen, however, African Americans and their allies had long struggled to achieve the rights promised them by the U.S. Constitution and its post-Civil War amendments. It is important also to understand that the modern civil rights movement rested on two pillars. One was formed by the brave nonviolent protesters who forced their fellow Americans at last to confront squarely the scandalous treatment of black Americans. The second consisted of attorneys such as Charles Hamilton Houston and his greatest student, Thurgood Marshall, who ensured that those protesters would have the United States' most powerful force — the law of the land — on their side.

Marshall, the attorney who argued for Montgomery's blacks in 1956, relied on legal precedents he had established in other successful court cases. *Brown v. Board of Education* was the most celebrated, but even before *Brown*, the partnership between Houston and Marshall had dismantled much of the legal structure by which the American South had enforced its Jim Crow system of race segregation.

Charles Hamilton Houston: The Man Who Killed Jim Crow

Charles Hamilton Houston was born in 1895 in Washington, D.C. A brilliant student, he graduated as a valedictorian from Amherst College at the age of 19, then served in a segregated U.S. Army unit during the First World War. After his brush with racism in the Army, Houston determined to make the fight for civil rights his life's calling. Returning home, he studied law at Harvard University, becoming the first African-American editor of its prestigious law review. He would go on to earn a PhD in juridical science at Harvard and a doctor of civil law degree at the University of Madrid in Spain.

Houston believed that an attorney's proper vocation was to wield the law as an instrument for securing justice. "A lawyer's either a social engineer or he's a parasite on society," he argued. In 1924, Houston began teaching part time at Howard University Law School, the Washington, D.C. institution responsible by some accounts for training fully three-fourths of the African-American attorneys then practicing. By 1929, Houston headed the law school.

In just six years, Houston radically improved the education of African-American law students, earned full accreditation for the school, and produced a group of lawyers trained in civil rights law. In the book *Black Profiles*, George R.

The skilled litigator and legal educator Charles Hamilton Houston launched the legal assault on "Jim Crow" laws.

Metcalf writes that Houston took the job to turn Howard into "a West Point [a popular name for the United States Military Academy] of Negro leadership, so that Negroes could gain equality by fighting segregation in the courts."

Meanwhile, the National Association for the Advancement of Colored People was laying the groundwork for a legal challenge to the separate-but-equal doctrine approved in the Supreme Court's 1896 *Plessy* decision. On Houston's recommendation, the organization engaged former U.S. Attorney Nathan Ross Margold to study the practical workings of separate but equal in the South. Margold's report — 218 legal-sized-pages long — was completed in 1931. It documented woeful inequality in state expenditures between white and black segregated schools.

In 1934, Houston accepted the position of NAACP special counsel. He surrounded himself with a select group of young, mostly Howard-trained lawyers, among them James Nabrit, Spottswood Robinson III, A. Leon Higginbotham, Robert Carter, William Hastie, George E.C. Hayes, Jack Greenberg, and Oliver Hill. With his young protégé Thurgood Marshall often in tow, Houston began to tour the South, armed with a camera and a portable typewriter. Marshall later recalled that he and Houston traveled in Houston's car: "There was no place to eat, no place to sleep. We slept in the car and we ate fruit." This could be dangerous work, but the visual record Houston compiled and the data amassed by Margold would anchor a new legal strategy: If the facilities allocated to blacks were not equal to those afforded whites, Houston reasoned, segregationist states were not meeting even the *Plessy* standard. Separate but equal logically required those states either to improve drastically the black facilities, a hugely expensive undertaking, or else integrate.

This equalization strategy bore fruit in 1935, when Houston and Marshall prevailed in a Maryland case, *Murray v. Pearson*. The African-American plaintiff challenged his rejection by the segregated University of Maryland law school. The university's lawyers argued that the school met the separate but equal requirement by granting qualified black applicants scholarships to enroll at out-of-state law schools. The state courts rejected this argument. While they were not yet prepared to rule against segregated public schools, they did hold that Maryland's out-of-state option was not an equal opportunity. Maryland's law school was ordered to admit qualified African-American students. The triumph was especially sweet for Marshall, who numbered himself among the qualified blacks rejected by the school.

Houston retired from the NAACP in 1940 because of ill health, and he died in 1950. "We owe it all to Charlie," Marshall later remarked. While Houston's prize student would lead the final legal assault on segregation, it was Houston, the teacher, who devised the strategy and illuminated the path.

Thurgood Marshall (left) and Charles Hamilton Houston flank Donald Gaines Murray, plaintiff in a case that struck the University of Maryland Law School policy denying admission to qualified black students.

Thurgood Marshall in 1962, after Senate confirmation of his appointment to the U.S. Court of Appeals. In 1967, President Lyndon B. Johnson appointed Marshall the first African-American Supreme Court justice.

Thurgood Marshall: Mr. Civil Rights

"No other American did more to lead our country out of the wilderness of segregation than Thurgood Marshall," said his fellow Supreme Court justice, Lewis Powell. Born in 1908 and educated in a segregated Baltimore, Maryland, secondary school, Marshall attended Lincoln University, "the first institution founded anywhere in the world to provide a higher education in the arts and sciences for youth of African descent." Knowing he would be turned away by the whites-only University of Maryland Law School, Marshall enrolled at Howard Law School, enduring the long commute from Baltimore to Washington, D.C. His mother pawned her wedding and engagement rings to pay the tuition. Marshall excelled at his studies, graduated first in his class of 1933, and earned the respect of Charles Hamilton Houston.

Working closely with Houston, Marshall prevailed in the *Murray v. Pearson* case described previously, then accepted a staff attorney position with the NAACP. In 1938, he succeeded Houston as head of the organization's legal committee. In 1940, he became the first chief of the NAACP Legal Defense Fund.

It was a wise choice. Marshall possessed a unique combination of skills. He was, as United Press International later concluded,

> ... an outstanding tactician with exceptional attention to detail, a tenacious ability to focus on a goal — and a deep voice that often was termed the loudest in the room. He also possessed a charm so extraordinary that even the most intransigent southern segregationist sheriff could not resist his stories and jokes.

Armed with this potent combination of likeability and skill, Thurgood Marshall in 1946 persuaded an all-white Southern jury to acquit 25 blacks of a rioting charge. On other occasions, he escaped only narrowly the beatings — or worse — risked by every assertive African American in the Jim Crow South.

It was under Marshall that the Houston-devised gradualist legal strategy at last succeeded. Case by case, Marshall and the NAACP attorneys chipped away at the legal pillars upholding segregation. In all, Marshall won an astounding 29 of the 32 cases he argued before the Supreme Court. His legal victories included the following:

- **Smith v. Allwright (1944)**, a Supreme Court decision barring the whites-only primary elections in which political parties chose their general election candidates. According to his biographer, Juan Williams, Marshall considered the case his most important triumph: "The segregationists would [demand that (the candidates) support segregation to capture their party's nomination], and by the time the blacks and Hispanics and ... even in some cases, the women, got to vote in the general election, they were just voting for one segregationist or the other; they didn't have a choice."
- **Morgan v. Virginia (1946)**, where Marshall obtained a Supreme Court ruling barring segregation in interstate bus transportation. In a later case, *Boynton v. Virginia* (1960), Marshall persuaded the court to order desegregation of bus terminals and other facilities made available to interstate passengers. These cases led to the Freedom Ride movement of the 1960s.
- In **Patton v. Mississippi (1947)**, the Supreme Court accepted Marshall's argument that juries from which African Americans had been systematically excluded could not convict African-American defendants.
- In **Shelley v. Kraemer (1948)**, Marshall persuaded the Supreme Court that state courts could not constitutionally prevent the sale of real property to blacks, even if that property was covered by a racially restrictive covenant. These covenants were a legal tactic commonly used to prevent homeowners from selling their properties to blacks, Jews, and other minorities.

The NAACP team's victories had established that the courts would overturn separate-but-equal arrangements where facilities were in fact not equal. It was a real achievement, but not the best tool to effect broad change, especially with regard to education. Poor African Americans in each of the hundreds of school districts in the South could hardly be expected to litigate the comparative merits of segregated black and white schools. Only a direct ruling against segregation itself could at one stroke eliminate disparities like those in Clarendon County, South Carolina, where per pupil expenditures in 1949-1950 averaged $179

Federal law often provided African Americans greater protection, but it typically applied only in an "interstate" context. Years before Rosa Parks, Irene Morgan refused to give up her seat on a bus whose route crossed state lines. With Thurgood Marshall as her attorney, Morgan prevailed, and segregation was legally barred on interstate bus routes.

Clockwise from top: President Dwight D. Eisenhower would use federal troops to ensure the enrollment of the first black students in the previously segregated Little Rock [Arkansas] Central High School.
The Revs. Martin Luther King Jr., Fred Shuttlesworth, and Ralph Abernathy confer.
A sign of progress: removal of a Jim Crow sign from a Greensboro, North Carolina, bus, 1956.

for white students and only $43 for blacks. Marshall would succeed in getting this direct ruling with the "case of the century," *Brown v. Board of Education*.

The *Brown* Decision

The *Brown* case began to take shape once Marshall found the right plaintiff in the Reverend Oliver Brown, father of Topeka, Kansas, grade-schooler Linda Brown. Linda had been obliged to attend a black school 21 blocks from her house, although there was a white school only seven blocks away. The Kansas state courts had rejected Brown's claim by finding that the segregated black and white schools were of comparable quality. This gave Marshall the chance to urge that the Supreme Court at last rule that segregated facilities were, by definition and as a matter of law, unequal and hence unconstitutional.

Marshall's legal strategy relied on social scientific evidence. The NAACP Legal Defense Fund assembled a team of experts spanning the fields of history, economics, political science, and psychology. Particularly significant was a study in which the psychologists Kenneth and Mamie Clark sought to determine how segregation affected the self-esteem and mental well-being of African Americans. Among their poignant findings: Black children aged three to seven preferred white rather than otherwise identical black dolls.

On May 17, 1954, a unanimous Supreme Court vindicated Marshall's strategy. Citing the Clark paper and other studies identified by plaintiffs, the Supreme Court ruled decisively:

> ... in the field of public education the doctrine of "separate but equal" has no place. Separate educational facilities are inherently unequal. Therefore, we hold that the plaintiffs and others similarly situated ... are, by reason of the segregation complained of, deprived of the equal protection of the laws guaranteed by the Fourteenth Amendment.

Education attorney Deryl W. Wynn, a member of the Oxford University Roundtable on Education Policy, has said of the significance of *Brown*:

> Here was the highest court in the land essentially saying that something was wrong with how black Americans were being treated.... I remember my father, who was a teenager at the time, saying the decision made him feel like he was somebody.... On a personal level, *Brown*'s real legacy is that it serves as a constant reminder that each child, each of us, is somebody.

The Court did not specify a timeframe for ending school segregation, but the following year, in a group of cases known collectively as "Brown II," Marshall and his colleagues secured a Supreme Court ruling that desegregation proceed "with all deliberate speed."

Even then, resistance continued in parts of the South. In September 1957, when black students were forcibly turned away from Central High School in Little Rock, Arkansas, Marshall flew to the city and filed suit in federal court. His victory in this case set the stage for President Dwight Eisenhower's declaration of September 24: "I have today issued an Executive Order directing the use of troops under federal authority to aid in the execution of federal law at Little Rock, Arkansas.... Mob rule cannot be allowed to override the decisions of our courts."

Brown, Little Rock, and the NAACP team's other legal triumphs illustrated both the strengths and the limits of the "legal" civil rights movement. Black Americans, relegated for decades to inferior, segregated schools, scarcely might have imagined the sight of federal authorities escorting black students into formerly all white classrooms — in Little Rock, at the University of Mississippi in 1962, and at the University of Alabama in 1963. But litigation worked slowly, and one case at a time.

Legal segregation, meanwhile, still prevailed in much of the South, not just at many schools but at nearly every kind of public facility, from swimming pools to buses and from movie theaters to lunch counters. And segregationists succeeded all too often in depriving African Americans of their most basic constitutional right. Through a combination of unfair technicalities, outright fraud and chicanery, and ultimately by threat of violence, the plain language of the Fifteenth Amendment was subverted, and blacks throughout the South were unable to vote.

Plainly, new civil rights laws were required. Passing them would require a political consensus strong enough to overcome the die-hard opposition of southern representatives in Congress. The legal struggle continued with Thurgood Marshall leading the way — from 1961 to 1965 as Judge Marshall of the U.S. Court of Appeals (the nation's second highest federal court), and then during the quarter-century from 1967 to 1991 as the nation's first African-American Supreme Court justice.

Meanwhile, a new, political civil rights movement was coalescing. Brave African Americans, joined by allies of every race and creed, began firmly but peaceably to insist upon the full measure of civil rights to which they were entitled as Americans. As they forced their countrymen to confront squarely the unconscionable realities of segregation and racial oppression, the balance of national sympathies — and of political forces — shifted. It all began on a December 1955 evening in Montgomery, Alabama, when a 42-year-old seamstress, tired after a long day at work, refused to give up her seat on a segregated bus.

RALPH JOHNSON BUNCHE:
SCHOLAR AND STATESMAN

Even as African Americans fought for their civil rights, their individual accomplishments demonstrated the justice of their cause. The achievements of the Nobel Prize-winning scholar and international official Ralph Bunche demonstrated to all fair-minded people that black Americans could contribute fully to American society.

Ralph Bunche was born in Detroit, Michigan, on August 7, 1903. His father was an itinerant barber, his mother a housewife and amateur pianist. His father abandoned the family, and his mother died when Bunche was 14 years old. From then on he lived in Los Angeles, California, with his maternal grandmother, whose wisdom and strength of character greatly influenced him. He graduated with honors from the University of California at Los Angeles and continued as a graduate student on scholarship at Harvard University.

From his earliest years, Bunche was acutely conscious of racial discrimination and was determined to work against it. His studies of colonial Africa persuaded him that colonialism had much in common with racial discrimination in the United States. He was determined to help put an end to both.

Dr. Ralph J. Bunche, peacemaker, mediator, and U.S. diplomat, receives the 1950 Nobel Prize for Peace.

Bunche set up the Political Science Department at Howard University, the historically black university in Washington, D.C. His many articles on racial discrimination later became basic literature for the U.S. civil rights movement. Bunche also pioneered the study of colonialism in the United States. He was the chief associate and co-writer of the Swedish social economist Gunnar Myrdal, whose landmark 1944 study of U.S. race relations, *An American Dilemma*, was cited approvingly by the U.S. Supreme Court in its *Brown v. Board of Education* decision.

As the Second World War loomed, Bunche was recruited by the U.S. government to advise on Africa, and then transferred to the State Department to work on the future United Nations charter. He was the first black official in the State Department. At the San Francisco Conference in 1945, he drafted two chapters of the charter, on non-self-governing territories (colonies) and on the trusteeship system. These chapters provided the basis for accelerating decolonization after the war. Bunche did as much as anyone to make decolonization a reality.

In the newly established United Nations, Bunche set up the trusteeship system. His achievements as a member of the U.N. Secretariat were extraordinary. As secretary of the 1947 U.N. Special Commission on Palestine, Bunche wrote the commission's majority report on partition as well as the minority report on a federal state. The former was adopted by the U.N. General Assembly and remains the basic goal of peacemakers in the Middle East.

In May 1948, the British left Palestine, a Jewish state was declared in that part of mandatory Palestine so designated by the General Assembly, and five Arab states invaded the new state of Israel. The U.N. Security Council appointed a mediator, Count Folke Bernadotte, with Bunche as his chief adviser. They established a truce in Palestine, and Bunche organized a group of U.N. military observers to supervise it, the beginning of U.N. peacekeeping operations. Bernadotte was assassinated by the Stern Gang (an armed, underground Zionist faction condemned by Bunche and by mainstream Zionists) in Jerusalem in September 1948, and Bunche became mediator. In January 1949, he initiated armistice talks, starting with Egypt and Israel. Armistice agreements were concluded between Israel and her four Arab neighbors, providing a formal basis for the cessation of hostilities. In 1950, Bunche won the Nobel Peace Prize for these achievements.

Dag Hammarskjold of Sweden became U.N. Secretary-General in 1953. As an undersecretary-general, Bunche became Hammarskjold's closest political adviser. In 1956 — after Egyptian nationalization of the Suez Canal — Britain, France, and Israel invaded Egypt in an ill-advised adventure that shocked the world. To get the invaders out of Egypt required something completely new, a U.N. "peace and police force," as its sponsor, Lester Pearson of Canada, called it. Hammarskjold asked Bunche to raise and deploy this force with minimum delay. Ominous Soviet threats of intervention lent additional urgency. Working around the clock with the enthusiastic support of the United States and many other countries, Bunche assembled and deployed the United Nations Emergency Force in Egypt only eight days after the General Assembly had called for it.

Bunche's pioneering effort in international peacekeeping was his proudest achievement. He set up and led the 20,000 strong U.N. peacekeeping operation dispatched to the Congo in 1960, and took the lead in forming a similar force in Cyprus in 1964. After Hammarskjold died in an air crash in Africa, Bunche became the indispensable adviser of Hammarskjold's successor, U Thant of Burma — so indispensable that U Thant's entreaties prevented Bunche from retiring from the United Nations to immerse himself full time in the civil rights movement. Bunche died, from overwork and the effects of diabetes, on December 9, 1971.

Ralph Bunche cared passionately about getting things done, but very little about getting personal credit. (He even tried to refuse the Nobel Peace Prize.) His great achievements are remembered, but seldom his role in them. African Americans, the millions liberated from the old colonial world, and the United Nations itself are particularly in his debt. He was one of the greatest public servants of the 20th century.

By **Brian Urquhart**
A former Undersecretary-General of the United Nations, Urquhart is the author of *Hammarskjöld*, *A Life in Peace and War*, *Ralph Bunche: An American Odyssey*, and other historical studies.

JACKIE ROBINSON:
BREAKING THE COLOR BARRIER

The Brooklyn Dodgers arrived at Shibe Park, bringing their new lightning rod of controversy to the baseball stadium in Philadelphia, Pennsylvania — a black player named Jackie Robinson. The symbols of intolerance flew down from the crowd, and the words of intolerance spilled out from the home team's bench. "Philadelphia was the worst," said Ralph Branca, who was there as a pitcher for Brooklyn. "They threw black cats on the field. They threw watermelon on the field. Ben Chapman, the Philadelphia manager, was very vocal, getting on Jackie."

It was 1947 in the United States, and for many the country still came in two shades — black and white. Some hearts, including many from the South, were long filled with hate simply over the color of a person's skin. Black people, from their perspective, didn't deserve equal civil rights with whites. And that had extended to the unofficial-but-understood idea among baseball officials and team owners since before the turn of the century that the major leagues were for white players only. Blacks would have to play on their own circuit, the Negro leagues.

But then came Robinson, bursting past the color barrier on April 15, 1947, as an infielder for the team in the racially diverse New York City borough of Brooklyn. He became a pioneering symbol that transcended sports, a large first step on a lengthy path toward driving home the concept of equality. His teammate Branca explained how Robinson's achievement transcended the baseball diamond:

> *I've often said that it changed baseball, but it also changed the country and eventually changed the world ..... Jackie made it easier for*

Top: After a Brooklyn victory over the New York Yankees in the first game of the 1952 World Series, Jackie Robinson (front right) celebrates with teammates Joe Black (back left), Duke Snyder (front left), and Pee Wee Reese (back right). Team manager Chuck Dressen is at center.
Above: Jackie Robinson (right) and former boxing heavyweight champion Floyd Patterson (left) meet in Birmingham, Alabama with civil rights leaders Ralph D. Abernathy and Martin Luther King Jr., 1963.

Rosa Parks. He made it easier for Martin Luther King Jr. And he made it easier for any black leader who was going to strive for racial equality. It basically changed the attitude of the whole country as far as looking at blacks.

It happened on the team. We had southern guys who grew up in that set of mores who looked down on blacks. They [African Americans] had to ride in the back of the bus, and they couldn't drink at the same water fountains, couldn't go to the same [bathrooms]. They [the white players] eventually changed their minds.

Born in Cairo, Georgia, on January 31, 1919, Robinson grew up in Pasadena, California. He excelled at four sports while in college at the nearby University of California at Los Angeles — baseball, football, basketball, and track. The U.S. Army drafted him in 1942. The military was still segregated (President Harry S. Truman would order its desegregation in 1948); when the proud Robinson refused to ride in the back of a bus, he was brought up on military charges of insubordination.

But he was acquitted and earned an honorable discharge. "He was a person of action," says his widow, Rachel Robinson. "He didn't want to be complacent about our situation."

Meanwhile, the Brooklyn Dodgers' general manager, Branch Rickey, decided it was time to integrate the national pastime of baseball, not least because he believed that African-American players would give his club a competitive advantage. Rickey understood that his man would have to possess the fortitude and strength of character to withstand the inevitable racist taunts — and worse — of players and fans. Rickey scouted Robinson in 1945, playing for Kansas City in the Negro leagues, and decided that he had found such a player, and such a man.

Robinson spent the next season with the Dodgers' minor-league team in Montreal, and then was promoted to the Dodgers for the 1947 season. It wasn't easy being a pioneer. Rickey made Robinson promise for three years not to respond to the insults that came at him from fans around the league and the opposing teams. Enduring pressure experienced by no player before or since, Robinson excelled on the field.

In his first major-league season, at the age of 28, Robinson played first base and compiled a .297 batting average. He displayed a dynamic style by stealing a National League-leading 29 bases, won the league's Rookie of the Year award, and helped the team reach the World Series. It helped that other teams acknowledged that Robinson had given the Dodgers a real edge and began themselves signing and playing black players. His best season came in 1949: He played second base and batted .342 with 16 home runs, 124 runs batted in, and 37 stolen bases, earning the league's Most Valuable Player award.

In all, Robinson spent 10 seasons with the Dodgers and made six World Series appearances, including Brooklyn's one and only championship year of 1955. After the following season, the six-time All-Star retired rather than go along with a trade to the rival New York Giants. In 1962, Robinson was inducted into the Baseball Hall of Fame, the first black player so honored.

After his playing career ended, Robinson continued to help in the fight for racial equality, speaking up for civil rights and for the leading men and organizations in the movement. This included service on the Board of Directors of the National Association for the Advancement of Colored People.

In 1972, Jackie Robinson suffered a heart attack and died, age 53. In those 53 years, Robinson impacted millions of lives. He shamed the bigot, inspired African Americans, and through his unflagging example of resilience and dignity moved Americans of all stripes toward acceptance of African-American civil rights.

"A life is not important," Robinson himself said, "except in the impact it has on other lives."

By **Brian Heyman**
The winner of over 30 journalism awards, Brian Heyman is a sportswriter at *The Journal-News* in White Plains, New York.

5
"We Have a Movement"

Above: Dr. King outlines strategies for the boycott of Montgomery, Alabama, buses. Among his advisors is Rosa Parks, seated second from left in the front row.
Left: After Rosa Parks refused to give up her bus seat, she was arrested, booked, and jailed. Her booking photo was discovered nearly a half-century later, during a house cleaning of the sheriff's office.

The successful boycott of segregated buses in Montgomery, Alabama — which began with the arrest of Rosa Parks on December 1, 1955 — transformed the civil rights cause into a mass political movement. It demonstrated that African Americans could unite and engage in disciplined political action, and marked the emergence of Martin Luther King Jr. — the indispensable leader who inspired millions, held them to the high moral standard of nonviolent resistance, and built bridges between Americans of all races, creeds, and colors. While many brave activists contributed to the civil rights revolution of the 1960s, it was King who, more than any other individual, forced millions of white Americans to confront directly the reality of Jim Crow — and shaped the political reality in which the landmark Civil Rights Act of 1964 and Voting Rights Act of 1965 could become law.

"Tired of Giving In": The Montgomery Bus Boycott

Rosa Parks would later say of the day that changed her life: "The only tired I was was tired of giving in." A secondary-school graduate at a time when diplomas were hard to come by for blacks in the South, Parks was active in her local NAACP, a registered voter (another privilege held by few southern blacks), and a respected figure in Montgomery, Alabama. In the summer of 1955, she attended an interracial leadership conference at the Highlander Folk School, a Tennessee institution that trained labor organizers and desegregation advocates. Parks thus knew of efforts to improve the lot of African Americans and that she was well-suited to provide a test case should the occasion arise.

On December 1, 1955, Parks was employed as a seamstress at a local department store. When she rode home from work that afternoon, she sat in the first row of the "colored section" of seats between the "white" and "black"

FREE AT LAST: THE U.S. CIVIL RIGHTS MOVEMENT 35

rows. When the white seats filled, the driver ordered Parks to give up her seat when another white person boarded the bus. Parks refused. She was arrested, jailed, and ultimately fined $10, plus $4 in court costs. Parks was 42 years old; she had crossed the line into direct political action.

An outraged black community formed the Montgomery Improvement Association (MIA) to organize a boycott of the city bus system. Partly to forestall rivalries among local community leaders, citizens turned to a recent arrival to Montgomery, the Reverend Martin Luther King Jr. The newly-installed pastor of the Dexter Avenue Baptist Church, King was just 26 years old but he had been born to leadership: His father, the Reverend Martin Luther King Sr., headed the influential Ebenezer Baptist Church in Atlanta, was active in the Georgia chapter of the NAACP, and had since the 1920s refused to ride Atlanta's segregated bus system.

In his first speech to MIA, the younger King told the group:

We have no alternative but to protest. For many years we have shown an amazing patience. We have sometimes given our white brothers the feeling that we liked the way we were being treated. But we come here tonight to be saved from that patience that makes us patient with anything less than freedom and justice.

Under King's leadership, boycotters organized carpools, while black taxi drivers charged boycotters the same fare — 10 cents — they would have paid on the bus. By auto, by horse-and-buggy, and even simply by walking, direct, nonviolent political action forced the city to pay a heavy economic price for its segregationist ways.

It also made a national figure of King, whose powerful presence and unsurpassed oratorical skills drew publicity for the movement and attracted support from sympathetic whites, especially those in the North. King, *Time* magazine later concluded, had "risen from nowhere to become one of the nation's remarkable leaders of men."

Even after his house was attacked and King himself, along with more than 100 boycotters, was arrested for "hindering a bus," his continued grace and adherence to nonviolent tactics earned respect for the movement and discredited the segregationists of Montgomery. When an explosion shook King's house with his wife and baby daughter inside, it briefly appeared that a riot would ensue. But King calmed the crowd:

We want to love our enemies — be good to them. This is what we must live by, we must meet hate with love. We must love our white brothers no matter what they do to us.

A white Montgomery policeman later told a journalist: "I'll be honest with you, I was terrified. I owe my life to that ... preacher, and so do all the other white people who were there."

In the end, the desegregation of the Montgomery bus system required not only Rosa Parks's personal initiative and bravery and King's political leadership, but also an NAACP-style legal effort. As the boycotters braved segregationist opposition, desegregationist attorneys cited the precedent of *Brown v. Board of Education* in their court challenge to the Montgomery bus ordinance. In November 1956, the Supreme Court of the United States rejected the city's final appeal, and the segregation of Montgomery buses ended. Thus fortified, the civil rights movement moved on to new battles.

Sit-Ins

Shortly after the successful conclusion of the Montgomery bus boycott, Martin Luther King and a number of senior movement figures — the Reverends Ralph Abernathy, T.J. Jemison, Joseph Lowery, Fred Shuttlesworth, and C.K. Steele, and the activists Ella Baker and Bayard Rustin — founded the Southern Christian Leadership Conference (SCLC). This new civil rights organization was devoted to a more aggressive approach than that of the legally oriented NAACP. The SCLC launched "Crusade for Citizenship," a voter registration effort.

Younger activists, meanwhile, were growing impatient with King's gradualist tactics. In 1960, some 200 of them, including Howard University student Stokley Carmichael, formed the Student Nonviolent Coordinating Committee, or SNCC. And in Greensboro, North Carolina, four freshman at the all-black North Carolina Agricultural and Technical College took matters into their own hands.

At 4:30 p.m. on February 1, 1960, students Ezell Blair Jr. (now Jibreel Khazan), Franklin Eugene McCain, Joseph Alfred McNeil, and David Leinail took whites-only seats at a local Woolworth department store lunch counter. They were denied service, but sat quietly until the store closed

A Montgomery, Alabama, sit-in, 1961. Merely by sitting quietly at segregated lunch counters, civil rights activists risked arrest ... and much worse.

The labor leader A. Philip Randolph (right) founded and led the Brotherhood of Sleeping Car Porters, which offered many African Americans a rare pathway to middle-class employment. Randolph's threatened 1941 march on Washington forced President Franklin D. Roosevelt to bar racial discrimination by defense contractors and served as the model for the famous 1963 march.

an hour later. The next morning, 20 Negro students took lunch-counter seats in groups of three or four. "There was no disturbance," the *Greensboro Record* reported, "and there appeared to be no conversation except among the groups. Some students pulled out books and appeared to be studying." Blair told the newspaper that Negro adults "have been complacent and fearful. ... It is time for someone to wake up and change the situation ... and we decided to start here."

The nonviolent occupation of a public space, or sit-in, dated at least to Mahatma Gandhi's campaigns for Indian independence from Britain. In the United States, labor organizations and the northern-based Congress of Racial Equality (CORE) had employed sit-ins as well. As events in Greensboro began to draw attention, SNCC moved swiftly to associate itself with this civil rights tactic, and over the next two months, sit-ins spread to more than 50 cities.

Particularly significant were events in Nashville, Tennessee, where the King-affiliated Nashville Christian Leadership Council had been preparing for this moment. Back in 1955, King had reached out to the Reverend James Lawson,

a civil rights activist and missionary who had served in India and studied Gandhian *satyagraha*, or nonviolent resistance. King urged Lawson to relocate to the South: "Come now," King said. "We don't have anyone like you down there."

Working with King's Southern Christian Leadership Conference, Lawson in 1958 began to train a new generation of nonviolent activists. His students included Diane Nash, James Bevel, and John Lewis, today a U.S. representative from Georgia. All soon would assume prominence in the civil rights movement. At these training seminars, they agreed to stage a series of sit-ins at department store restaurants. Blacks were permitted to spend money in those stores, but not to eat at their restaurants.

The Nashville activists organized carefully and moved deliberately. But when the Greensboro sit-in began to draw national attention, they were ready. In February 1960, hundreds of their activists began the sit-ins. Their student-drafted instruction sheets captured the personal discipline and dignified commitment to nonviolence they would offer the world:

Don't strike back or curse back if abused. ... Don't block entrances to the stores and aisles.

Show yourself friendly and courteous at all times.

Sit straight and always face the counter. ...

Remember the teachings of Jesus Christ, Mohandas K. Gandhi, and Martin Luther King.

Remember love and nonviolence, may God bless each of you.

Typically a lunch counter would close when a sit-in began, but after the first few incidents, police began to arrest protestors, and the subsequent trials drew large crowds. When convicted of disorderly conduct, the activists chose to serve jail time rather than pay a fine.

Nashville was an early example of how Jim Crow could not survive exposure. The legendary journalist David Halberstam was just beginning his career, and his reports for the *Nashville Tennessean* helped attract national media attention. The sit-in movement spread throughout much of the country, and soon Americans across the nation were stunned by photographs like the one that appeared in the February 28, 1960 *New York Times*. The caption read: "A white man swings an 18-inch-long [46-centimeter-long] bat at a Negro woman in Montgomery. She was injured by the blow. The attack occurred yesterday after the woman brushed against another white man. Police, standing near by, made no arrest."

On April 19 of that year, a bomb exploded at the home of the Nashville students' chief legal counsel. Some 2,000 African Americans swiftly organized a march to the City Hall, where they confronted the mayor. Would he, Diane Nash asked, favor ending lunch-counter segregation? Yes, came the reply, but, "I can't tell a man how to run his business. He has got rights too."

This "right" to discriminate lay at the heart of the struggle. Meanwhile, the bad publicity stung the businessmen of Nashville, as did the stark contrast between the dignified, nonviolent black students and their armed and all-too-violent opponents. Secret negotiations began, and on May 10, 1960, quietly and without fanfare, a number of downtown lunch counters began serving black customers. There were no further incidents, and soon thereafter Nashville became the first southern city successfully to begin desegregating its public facilities.

Freedom Rides

Some of the young Nashville sit-in leaders joined up with the Student Nonviolent Coordinating Committee, which in 1961 helped to launch the "Freedom Rides." Back in 1946, Thurgood Marshall's NAACP lawyers had obtained a Supreme Court ruling that barred segregation in interstate bus travel. (Under the U.S. federal system of government, it is easier for the national government to regulate commerce that crosses state lines.) In the 1960 *Boynton v. Virginia* decision, the Court expanded its ruling to include bus terminals and other facilities associated with interstate travel. But possessing a right and exercising it are two very different things.

It was widely understood that any African American who exercised his or her constitutional right to sit at the front of an interstate bus or use the previously whites-only facilities at a southern bus terminal would meet with a violent response. Understanding this, an interracial group of 13, including CORE National Director James Farmer, departed Washington, D.C., by bus. Farmer and his companions planned to make several stops en route to New Orleans. "If there is arrest, we will accept that arrest," Farmer said. "And if there is violence, we are willing to receive that violence without responding in kind."

Farmer was right to anticipate violence. Perhaps the worst of it occurred near Anniston, Alabama. Departing Atlanta, the Freedom Riders had split into two groups, one riding in a Greyhound bus, the other in a Trailways bus. When the Greyhound bus reached Anniston, the sidewalks, unusually, were lined with people. The reason soon became clear. When the bus reached the station parking lot, a mob set upon it, using rocks and brass knuckles to shatter some of the bus windows. Two white highway patrolmen in the bus, assigned to spy on the Riders, sealed the door and prevented the Ku Klux Klan-led mob from entering.

When the local police finally arrived, they bantered with the crowd, made no arrests, and escorted the bus to the city limits. The mob, by some accounts now about 200 strong, followed close behind in cars and pickup trucks. About 10 kilometers outside Anniston, flat tires brought the bus to a halt. A crowd of white men attempted to board the bus, and one threw a fire bomb through a bus window. As the historian Raymond Arsenault writes: "The Freedom Riders had been all but doomed until an exploding fuel tank convinced the mob that the whole bus was about to explode." The bus was consumed by the blaze; the fleeing Freedom Riders, reported the Associated Press, "took a brief but bloody beating."

Boarding a June, 1961 Freedom Ride from Washington, D.C., to Florida are the Rev. Perry A. Smith III, of Brentwood, Maryland, and Rev. Robert Stone of New York City.
Left: A Trailways bus with Freedom Riders aboard approaches the bus terminal in Jackson, Mississippi.

Freedom Riders traveling from Montgomery, Alabama, to Jackson, Mississippi, are escorted by National Guardsmen with bayonets at the ready. Over 20 additional Freedom Riders are behind the guardsmen.

The second group of Freedom Riders shared their Trailways bus with a group of Klansmen who boarded at Atlanta. When the black Freedom Riders refused to sit at the back of the bus, more beatings ensued. The white Freedom Riders, among them 61-year-old educator Walter Bergman, were attacked with particular savagery. All of the Freedom Riders held to their Ghandian training; none fought back. When the bus at last arrived in Birmingham, matters only grew worse. CBS News commentator Howard K. Smith offered an eyewitness account: "When the bus arrived, the toughs grabbed the passengers into alleys and corridors, pounding them with pipes, with key rings, and with fists." Inside the segregated bus station, the Freedom Riders hesitated momentarily, then entered the whites-only waiting room. They, too, were beaten, some unconscious, while Birmingham's police chief, Eugene "Bull" Connor, refused to restrain the Klansmen and their supporters.

Still, the Riders were determined to continue. In Washington, Attorney General Robert F. Kennedy asked Alabama Governor John Patterson to guarantee safe passage through his state. Patterson declined: "The citizens of the state are so enraged I cannot guarantee protection for this bunch of rabble-rousers." A member of Alabama's congressional delegation, Representative George Huddleston Jr., deemed the Freedom Riders "self-anointed merchants of racial hatred." He said the firebombed Greyhound group "got just what they asked for."

In Nashville, Diane Nash feared the political consequences. "If the Freedom Ride had been stopped as a result of violence," she later said, "I strongly felt that the future of the movement was going to be just cut short because

the impression would have been given that whenever a movement starts, that all that has to be done is that you attack it with massive violence and the blacks would stop." With reinforcements from the Student Nonviolent Coordinating Committee and other black and white activists supplementing the original Freedom Riders, a new effort was launched.

On May 20, a group of Freedom Riders boarded a Birmingham-to-Montgomery, Alabama, Greyhound. Their bus was met by a mob estimated at 1,000 "within an instant" of pulling into the station, the Associated Press reported. Among the injured were John Seigenthaler, an assistant to Attorney General Kennedy. Kennedy dispatched 400 federal marshals to Montgomery to enforce order, while the Congress of Racial Equality promised to continue the Freedom Ride, pressing on to Jackson, Mississippi, and then to New Orleans. "Many students are standing by in other cities to serve as volunteers if needed," James Farmer told the *New York Times*. And some 450 Americans did step forward, boarding the buses and then filling the jails, notably in Jackson, when Farmer and others refused to pay fines imposed for "breaching the peace."

On May 29, Attorney General Kennedy directed the Interstate Commerce Commission to adopt stiff regulations to enforce the integration of interstate transportation. The agency did so. With this sustained federal effort, Jim Crow faltered in bus terminals, on buses, and on trains, at least those that crossed state lines.

The Freedom Riders' victory set the tone for the great civil rights campaigns that followed. Not for the first time during these climactic years, a free press forced Americans to take a cold, hard look at the reality of racial oppression. The Birmingham mob beat Tommy Langston, a photographer for the local *Post-Herald* newspaper, and smashed his camera. But they forgot to remove the film, and the newspaper's front page subsequently displayed his picture of the savage beating of a black bystander. Each arrest and each beating attracted more media and more coverage. And while many of those accounts still referred to "Negro militants," the contrast between rabid white mobs and the calm, dignified, biracial Freedom Riders forced Americans to decide, or at this point at least begin deciding: Who best represented American values?

White religious leaders were prominent among those who lauded the bravery of the Freedom Riders and the justice of their cause. The Reverend Billy Graham called for prosecution of their attackers and declared it "deplorable when certain people in any society have been treated as second-class citizens." Rabbi Bernard J. Bamberger denounced white segregationist violence as "utterly indefensible in terms of morality and law" and criticized whites who urged civil rights activists to "go slow." And always there were the righteous: Raymond Arsenault writes that while the Greyhound bus burned outside Anniston, "one little girl, 12-year-old Janie Miller, supplied the choking victims with water, filling and refilling a five-gallon [19-liter] bucket while braving the insults and taunts of Klansmen."

The Albany Movement

Two major civil rights campaigns during 1962 and 1963 would illustrate both the limits and the possibilities of nonviolent resistance. African Americans in the segregated city of Albany, Georgia, had traditionally engaged in as much political activism as was possible in the Jim Crow South. In 1961, SNCC volunteers arrived to beef up an ongoing voter registration effort. They established a voter-registration center that served as a home base for a campaign of sit-ins, boycotts, and other protests. In November 1961, a number of local black organizations formed the Albany Movement, under the leadership of William G. Anderson, a young osteopath. The protests accelerated, and by mid-December more than 500 demonstrators had been jailed. Anderson had met both Martin Luther King Jr. and his colleague, the Reverend Ralph Abernathy, pastor at Montgomery's First Baptist Church and King's chief lieutenant at the Southern Christian Leadership Conference. He decided to invite King's help, both to maintain the Albany Movement's momentum and to secure national publicity for its cause.

Albany Police Chief Laurie Pritchett proved a formidable opponent for King and the other activists. Pritchett realized that news media coverage of segregationist violence against dignified, nonviolent civil rights activists already had turned many Americans against Jim Crow. Pritchett worked assiduously to deprive the Albany Movement of a similar "media moment." Albany police officers were warned against employing any kind of violence against protestors, especially if the press was nearby. While earlier protestors had successfully "filled the jails," Pritchett scattered them in jails throughout the surrounding counties. "In the end," the *New Georgia Encyclopedia* concluded, "King ran out of willing marchers before Pritchett ran out of jail space."

Pritchett also understood that King was the media star and that national press coverage would ebb if there was no King "angle" to pursue. King returned several times to Albany, and several times was arrested and convicted for breach of

Montgomery, Alabama: about 70 clergymen of different creeds and denominations being arrested after holding an anti-segregation prayer vigil in front of city hall, August 1962.

the peace. When the court offered King and Abernathy their choice of jail time or a fine, they chose jail, the option certain to attract press coverage. But they found that an "anonymous benefactor" — a segregationist recruited by Pritchett — had paid their fine.

When the media moment finally came, it was not the one King had hoped for. By July 24, 1962, many of Albany's African Americans had grown frustrated at the lack of progress. That evening, a crowd of 2,000 blacks armed with bricks, bottles, and rocks attacked a group of Albany policemen and Georgia highway patrolmen. One trooper lost two teeth. But Laurie Pritchett's well-schooled officers did not retaliate, and the chief was quick to seize the initiative: "Did you see them nonviolent rocks?" he asked.

King moved swiftly to limit the damage. He cancelled a planned mass demonstration and declared a day of penance. But a federal injunction against further demonstrations in Albany added to the difficulties: Up till then, the civil rights cause had had the law on its side. Further action in Albany would allow segregationists to portray King and his followers as lawbreakers.

King understood that his presence in Albany would no longer help the wider movement. SNCC, NAACP, CORE, and other local activists continued the fight in Albany and would eventually secure real gains for the city's African Americans. For King and his SCLC team, Albany was a learning experience. As King explained in his autobiography:

When we planned our strategy for Birmingham months later, we spent many hours assessing Albany and trying to learn from its errors. Our appraisals not only helped to make our subsequent tactics more effective, but revealed that Albany was far from an unqualified failure.

Arrest in Birmingham

If Albany Police Chief Laurie Pritchett possessed the political savvy and emotional detachment to fight nonviolence with nonviolence, his Birmingham, Alabama, counterpart, Bull Connor, did not. King and the other movement leaders rightly anticipated that Connor would prove a perfect foil. King biographer Marshall Frady depicted Connor as "a bombastic segregationist of the old, unapologetically bluff sort — a podgy, strutful, middle-aged bossman in a snap-brim straw hat who ... held a famously irascible temper." Connor did not represent the views of all white Birmingham residents; a recent municipal election had produced gains for reformist candidates. But he controlled the police, and the "greeting" that the Freedom Riders had experienced in Birmingham amply illustrated what activists might expect to find there.

Albany had taught King and his SCLC team to focus on specific goals rather than a general desegregation. As King later wrote:

We concluded that in hard-core communities, a more effective battle could be waged if it was concentrated against one aspect of the evil and intricate system of segregation. We decided, therefore, to center the Birmingham struggle on the business community, for we knew that the Negro population had sufficient buying power so that its withdrawal could make the difference between profit and loss for many businesses.

Albany, Georgia: African-American demonstrators kneel in prayer during a December 1961 hearing for Freedom Riders arrested there.

On April 3, 1963, activists launched a round of lunch-counter sit-ins. A march on Birmingham's City Hall followed on the 6th. The city's African Americans began to boycott downtown businesses, a tactic King deemed "amazingly effective." A number of shops swiftly removed their whites-only signs, only to be threatened by Bull Connor with the loss of their business licenses. As the numbers of volunteers grew, the Birmingham movement expanded its efforts to "kneel-ins" in local church buildings and library sit-ins. The number of arrests grew and the jails filled.

The police response remained muted to this point. *The New York Times* described a typical incident:

Eight Negros entered the segregated library. They strolled through three of the four floors and sat at desks reading magazines and books. The police were present but did not order them to leave. They left voluntarily after about half an hour.

About 25 whites were in the library when the Negroes entered. Some made derogatory remarks such as, "It stinks in here." Others asked the Negroes: "Why don't you go home?" But there were no incidents.

On April 10, Connor followed Pritchett's example, obtaining a county court injunction barring King, Fred Shuttlesworth, and 134 other leaders from engaging in boycotts, sit-ins, picketing, and other protest activities. Any violation of the injunction would be contempt of court, punishable by more substantial jail time than a mere breach of peace.

King now faced a choice. He and Abernathy decided they would violate the injunction. King issued a brief statement:

We cannot in all good conscience obey such an injunction which is an unjust, undemocratic, and unconstitutional misuse of the legal process.

We do this not out of any disrespect for the law but out of the highest respect for the law. This is not an attempt to evade or defy the law or engage in chaotic anarchy. Just as in all good conscience we cannot obey unjust laws, neither can we respect the unjust use of the courts.

We believe in a system of law based on justice and morality. Out of our great love for the Constitution of the United States and our desire to purify the judicial system of the state of Alabama, we risk this critical move with an awareness of the possible consequences involved.

On Good Friday, April 12, 1963, Martin Luther King led a protest march toward downtown Birmingham. On the fifth block, King, Abernathy, and about 60 others, including a white clergyman who joined the protest, were arrested. As King was taken into custody, Connor remarked: "That's what he came down here for, to get arrested. Now he's got it."

Letter From Birmingham Jail

As King languished in his jail cell, he produced one of the most extraordinary documents in the history of American thought. A number of local white clergymen, themselves friendly to King's long-term objectives, disagreed with his short-term tactics. They published a public statement calling the King-led demonstrations "unwise and untimely," and they opposed King's civil disobedience "however technically peaceful those actions may be."

King's reply was the *Letter From Birmingham Jail*. Lacking writing paper, he scribbled in the margins of a newspaper page. King's handwritten words wrapped around the pest control ads and garden club news, recalled the King aide who smuggled the newsprint out of the jail. Yet those margins held a powerful condemnation of inaction in the face of injustice, and they displayed an extraordinary faith that in America the cause of freedom necessarily would prevail.

King answered the white pastors' charges with timeless, universal truth. Accused of being an outsider fomenting tension in Birmingham, King replied that, in the face of oppression, there were no outsiders. "Injustice anywhere is a threat to justice everywhere. We are caught in an inescapable network of mutuality, tied in a single garment of destiny. Whatever affects one directly, affects all indirectly." As for the tension: "There is a type of constructive, nonviolent tension which is necessary for growth." For those who do not themselves suffer from the disease of segregation, King added, no direct action ever seems well timed: " 'Wait' has almost always meant 'Never.'" No man, he continued, can "set the timetable for another man's freedom."

Acknowledging that he and his followers had indeed violated the county court injunction, King cited Saint Augustine's distinction between just and unjust laws. He asserted that one who breaks an unjust law in order to arouse the consciousness of his community "is in reality expressing the highest respect for law," provided he acts "openly, lovingly, and with a willingness to accept the penalty." Writing from his cell, King led by example.

From that cell, King believed that in the United States, freedom ultimately would —indeed, must — prevail: "I have no fear about the outcome of our struggle. ... We will reach the goal of freedom ... because the goal of America is freedom. ... Our destiny is tied up with America's destiny ... the sacred heritage of our nation and the eternal will of God are embodied in our echoing demands. ... One day," King concluded, "the South will recognize its real heroes."

"We Have a Movement"

Because the Birmingham campaign required their leadership, Martin Luther King Jr. and Ralph Abernathy posted bond after eight days in jail. They turned to an idea credited to the Reverend James Bevel, a Nashville sit-in and Freedom Ride veteran recruited by King to serve as Southern Christian Leadership Conference's director of direct action and nonviolent education. Knowing that few black families could afford to have their primary wage earner serve jail time, Bevel began to organize the city's young African Americans. College students, secondary schoolers, and even elementary school pupils were instructed in the principles of nonviolence. They prepared to march downtown, there to enter whites-only lunch counters, use the whites-only drinking fountains, study in the whites-only libraries, pray in the whites-only churches. In some denominations, at least, white churches welcomed the young blacks.

The decision to use children was a controversial one. The SCLC's executive director, the Reverend Wyatt Tee Walker, defended it on the grounds that "Negro children will get a better education in five days in jail than in five months in a segregated school." In his *Autobiography*, King related the case of a black teenager who decided to march in the face of his father's objections:

"Daddy," the boy said, "I don't want to disobey you, but I have made my pledge. If you try to keep me home, I will sneak off. If you think I deserve to be punished for that, I'll just have to take the punishment. For, you see, I'm not doing this only because I want to be free. I'm doing it also because I want freedom for you and Mama, and I want it to come before you die."

That father thought again, and gave his son his blessing.

On May 2, 1963, hundreds of young African Americans set out, linked by walkie-talkie, singing "We Shall Overcome." Hundreds were arrested, swelling the Birmingham jail well beyond its capacity. Perhaps most importantly, they stretched Bull Connor's temper to its breaking point.

On May 3, Connor determined to halt the demonstrations by force. Fire hoses set to full pressure — enough to peel bark from a tree — knocked protestors off their feet and rolled them down the asphalt streets. At the police chief's order, police dogs were used to disperse the crowds, and several demonstrators were bitten.

Student Nonviolent Coordinating Committee activist James Foreman was at SCLC headquarters when the news came. He reported that the leaders there were "jumping up and down, elated. ... They said over and over again, 'We've got a movement. We've got a movement. We had some police brutality.' " Foreman thought this "very cold, cruel, and calculating," but, as the historian C. Vann Woodward concluded: "The more seasoned campaigners had learned the price and worth of photographic opportunities."

The young demonstrators returned each day that week, as did the hoses and the dogs. The resulting photographs, video, and written accounts dominated the news in the United States and in much of the world. Faced with the greatest provocation, most demonstrators remained nonviolent. James Bevel roamed the streets, shouting through a bullhorn: "If you're not going to demonstrate in a nonviolent way, then leave." By May 6, Bull Connor was housing thousands of child prisoners at the state fairgrounds.

A *New York Times* editorial expressed the feeling of growing numbers of Americans:

> No American schooled in respect for human dignity can read without shame of the barbarities committed by Alabama police authorities against Negro and white demonstrators for civil rights. The use of police dogs and high-pressure fire hose to subdue schoolchildren in Birmingham is a national disgrace. The herding of hundreds of teenagers and many not yet in their teens into jails and detention homes for demanding their birthright of freedom makes a mockery of legal process.

In Washington, D.C., one very important reader shared this sentiment. As King biographer Marshall Frady relates:

> One news photo of a policeman clutching the shirtfront of a black youth with one hand while his other held the leash of a dog swirling at the youth's midsection happened to pass under the eyes of the president in the Oval Office, and he told a group of visitors that day, "It makes me sick."

On May 7, Fred Shuttlesworth was injured by a fire hose stream that hurled him against the side of his church. Arriving

Birmingham, Alabama, May 1963: Fire hoses set to full pressure could strip the bark from a tree. Sheriff Bull Connor ordered their use against non-violent civil rights protestors and a horrified nation watched.

a few minutes later, Bull Connor declared: "I'm sorry I missed it. ... I wish they'd carried him away in a hearse."

By May 9, Birmingham's business leaders had had enough. They negotiated an agreement with King and Shuttlesworth. Birmingham businesses would desegregate their lunch counters, restrooms, and drinking fountains. They would hire and promote black employees. The jailed protestors would be freed, and charges dropped. Bull Connor called it "the worst day of my life."

The triumph of the Birmingham movement reflected the bravery and discipline of the African-American protestors. It spoke to the inspiring and hard-headed leadership of men like Martin Luther King Jr., Ralph Abernathy, Fred Shuttlesworth, James Bevel, and others. It forced Americans to confront squarely — in their newspapers and on their television screens — the reality of Jim Crow brutality. And it reflected an idealism that had survived both slavery and segregation, and also an impatience over promises long deferred. On May 8, a Birmingham juvenile court judge conducted a hearing on the case of a 15-year-old boy arrested during the May 3 demonstrations:

> JUDGE: *I often think of what the Founding Fathers said: "There is no freedom without restraint." Now I want you to go home and go back to school. Will you do that?*
>
> BOY: *Can I say something?*
>
> JUDGE: *Anything you like.*
>
> BOY: *Well, you can say that because you've got your freedom. The Constitution says we're all equal, but Negroes aren't equal.*
>
> JUDGE: *But you people have made great gains and they still are. It takes time.*
>
> BOY: *We've been waiting over 100 years.*

The March on Washington

Birmingham was a real victory, but a costly one. The long-term solution could not be for African Americans to defeat segregation one city at a time or by absorbing beatings, dog bites, and hosings. Even as the civil rights movement scored real gains, each advance came over dogged opposition. Federal troops were needed to ensure the admission of James Meredith, the first black to study at the University of Mississippi, in 1962. The following year, Alabama's governor, George Wallace, whose inaugural address promised "segregation now, segregation tomorrow, segregation forever," staged a "stand in the schoolhouse door." Only the intervention of federal marshals ensured the enrollment of African Americans Vivian Malone and James Hood at the University of Alabama. The very next day, Medgar Evers, leader of the Mississippi NAACP, was murdered outside his home in Jackson. And in Birmingham itself, on September 15, 1963, three Klansmen planted 19 sticks of dynamite in the basement of the Sixteenth Street Baptist Church, the unofficial headquarters of the Birmingham movement. Four young girls — Addie Mae Collins, Carole Robertson, Cynthia Wesley, and Denise McNair — were killed and 22 injured.

On June 11, 1963, President John F. Kennedy told the nation that he would submit to Congress legislation prohibiting segregation in all privately owned facilities: hotels, restaurants, theaters, retail stores, and the like. "We are confronted primarily," the president said, "with a moral issue. It is as old as the scriptures and as clear as the American Constitution." But the obstacles to passage of effective civil rights laws remained imposing.

A number of black leaders were determined to change the political reality in which members of Congress would consider civil rights legislation. One was A. Philip Randolph. Now well into his 70s, Randolph had earlier organized and for decades led the Brotherhood of Sleeping Car Porters union. African Americans had long supplied large numbers of rail car attendants. These were among the best jobs open to blacks in much of the country, and Randolph, as leader of these porters, had emerged as an important figure in the American labor movement.

Back in 1941, President Franklin D. Roosevelt had sought to boost defense production in anticipation of possible U.S. entry into the Second World War. Randolph confronted Roosevelt, demanding an end to segregation in federal government agencies and among defense contractors. Otherwise, Randolph warned, he would launch a massive protest march on Washington, D.C. Roosevelt soon issued an executive order barring discrimination in defense industries and federal bureaus and creating the Fair Employment Practices Committee. After the war, pressure from Randolph contributed to President Harry S Truman's 1948 order desegregating the American armed forces.

Now Randolph and his talented assistant Bayard Rustin contemplated a similar march, hoping "to embody in one gesture civil rights as well as national economic demands." A "Big Six" group of civil rights leaders was formed to organize the event. Included were Randolph, King, Roy Wilkins (representing the National Association for the Advancement of Colored People), James Farmer (Congress of Racial Equality), John Lewis (Student Nonviolent Coordinating Committee), and Whitney Young Jr. (Urban League). They fixed a date: August 28, 1963, and site for the main rally: the Lincoln Memorial in Washington, D.C.

The "March on Washington for Jobs and Freedom" would be the largest political demonstration the nation had ever seen. Chartered buses and trains carried participants from throughout the nation. A quarter-million Americans, and by some estimates even more, gathered that day, among them at least 50,000 whites. On the podium stood a stellar assemblage of civil rights champions, Christian and Jewish religious leaders, labor chiefs, and entertainers. The black contralto Marian Anderson, who had performed at the Lincoln Memorial in 1939 after being refused permission to sing at Washington's Constitution Hall, offered the national anthem. Each of the Big Six addressed the crowd that day, except for Farmer, who had been arrested during a protest in Louisiana.

The best-remembered moment would be King's. Considered by many the finest oration ever delivered by an American, King's "I Have a Dream" speech drew on themes from the Bible and from such iconic American texts as the Constitution, the Declaration of Independence, and Abraham Lincoln's Gettysburg Address. King organized his remarks in the style and structure of a sermon, the kind he had delivered at many a Sunday morning church service.

The speech began by linking the civil rights cause to earlier promises unfulfilled. Lincoln's Emancipation Proclamation, King said, appeared to the freed slaves as "a joyous daybreak to end the long night of their captivity." But 100 years later, he continued, "the Negro ... finds himself an exile in his own land." When the nation's founders wrote the Declaration of Independence and the Constitution, "they were signing a promissory note to which every American was to fall heir. This note was a promise that all men, yes, black men as well as white men, would be guaranteed the 'unalienable rights' of 'life, liberty, and the pursuit of happiness.' "

America, King continued, had defaulted on that promissory note, at least to her citizens of color.

> *We refuse to believe that the bank of justice is bankrupt. We refuse to believe that there are insufficient funds in the great vaults of opportunity of this nation. And so, we've come to*

The "Big Six" meet in New York to plan the March on Washington. Left to right: John Lewis, Whitney Young, A. Philip Randolph, Martin Luther King Jr., James Farmer, and Roy Wilkins.

cash this check, a check that will give us upon demand the riches of freedom and the security of justice.

"There will be neither rest nor tranquility in America until the Negro is granted his citizenship rights," King warned, but he also noted that

> in the process of gaining our rightful place, we must not be guilty of wrongful deeds. Let us not seek to satisfy our thirst for freedom by drinking from the cup of bitterness and hatred. We must forever conduct our struggle on the high plane of dignity and discipline. We must not allow our creative protest to degenerate into physical violence.

Some believe that King spoke extemporaneously as he delivered the "dream" portion of his address. The famed gospel singer Mahalia Jackson was on the stage while King spoke, and she addressed him during the speech: "Tell them about the dream, Martin," she said. And he did.

> ... and so even though we face the difficulties of today and tomorrow, I still have a dream. It is a dream deeply rooted in the American dream.

> I have a dream that one day this nation will rise up and live out the true meaning of its creed: "We hold these truths to be self-evident, that all men are created equal."

> I have a dream that one day on the red hills of Georgia, the sons of former slaves and the sons of former slave owners will be able to sit down together at the table of brotherhood.

> I have a dream that one day even the state of Mississippi, a state sweltering with the heat of injustice, sweltering with the heat of oppression, will be transformed into an oasis of freedom and justice.

> I have a dream that my four little children will one day live in a nation where they will not be judged by the color of their skin but by the content of their character.

I have a dream today!

As the words and images of the day's events sped across the nation and around the world, momentum for real change accelerated. But there were battles still to be fought, and victory, while ever closer, still lay in the distance.

"I have a dream today!" Martin Luther King addresses the largest political demonstration the nation had ever seen. For many, his speech in 1963 was the finest ever delivered by an American.

FREE AT LAST: THE U.S. CIVIL RIGHTS MOVEMENT 45

ROSA PARKS:
MOTHER OF THE CIVIL RIGHTS MOVEMENT

Rosa McCauley Parks is known today as the "mother of the civil rights movement" because her arrest for refusing to give up her bus seat sparked the pivotal Montgomery, Alabama, bus boycott. She didn't set out to make history when she left her job as a seamstress to board a bus on the afternoon of December 1, 1955. She was tired, and she just wanted to go home. Still, when the bus driver asked her to move toward the back of the bus so that a white man could sit, she couldn't bring herself to do it.

"I didn't get on the bus with the intention of being arrested," she said later. "I got on the bus with the intention of going home."

While she did not know her act would set in motion a 381-day bus boycott, she knew one thing. Her own personal bus boycott began that day.

"I knew that as far as I was concerned, I would never ride on a segregated bus again."

The arrest and brief jailing of Rosa Parks, a woman highly respected in the black community, and the boycott that followed led to a U.S. Supreme Court decision outlawing segregation on city buses. The boycott also raised to national prominence a youthful, little-known minister named Martin Luther King Jr. Under his leadership, the boycott set a

Above: Rosa Parks seated at the front of the bus, after the Supreme Court of the United States ruled unconstitutional the segregated seating that had prevailed on the Montgomery, Alabama, bus system. Parks's December 1955 refusal to give up her seat to a white man sparked the Montgomery Bus Boycott and launched the civil rights career of Martin Luther King Jr. Right: Rosa Parks being fingerprinted after her arrest.

pattern for nonviolent, community-based protest that became a successful strategy in the civil rights movement.

There were many forces in Rosa Parks's early life that helped forge her quiet activism. She was born Rosa Louise McCauley on February 4, 1913, in Tuskegee, Alabama. Her childhood revolved around a small church where her uncle was the pastor. There she developed both a strong faith and a sense of racial pride. Parks later in life spoke proudly of the fact that the African Methodist Episcopal Church had for generations been a strong advocate for black equality.

She also was strongly influenced by her grandparents, especially her grandfather. He responded to the family's fears of the violent, racist, secret society known as the Ku Klux Klan by keeping a loaded double-barreled shotgun nearby. While the very real possibility of Klan violence never materialized for her immediate family, her grandfather's defiant attitude helped mold her thinking.

When she turned 11, Rosa was sent to a school for girls in Montgomery that had an all-black student body and an all-white teaching staff.

At the school, Parks learned "to believe we could do what we wanted in life." She also learned from the teachers that not all white people were bigots.

It was there she met Johnnie Carr, and the two girls started a friendship that would last a lifetime. Carr said of her friend's childhood: "I was noisy and talkative, but she was very quiet, and always stayed out of trouble. But whatever she did, she always put herself completely into it. But she was so quiet you would never have believed she would get to the point of being arrested."

Parks wanted to be a teacher, but had to drop out of school to care for her ailing mother. (She later received her high school diploma.) When she was 18, she fell in love with barber Raymond Parks and they later married. During part of the Second World War, she worked at the racially desegregated Maxwell Field (now Maxwell Air Force Base) in Montgomery. She later attributed her indignation toward the segregated Montgomery transportation system to the contrast with the integrated on-base transportation she had experienced.

After the bus boycott ended successfully in 1956, Parks continued working for civil rights. On several occasions she joined King to support his efforts. The following year, Parks moved north, to Detroit, Michigan, where she worked for Congressmen John Conyers, who often joked that he had more people visit his office to meet his staff assistant than to meet him.

Parks was inducted into the National Women's Hall of Fame in 1993. She was presented the Medal of Freedom Award by President Bill Clinton in 1996 and the Congressional Gold Medal in 1999. The Southern Christian Leadership Council established an annual Rosa Parks Freedom Award.

After her death on October 24, 2005, Congress approved a resolution allowing her body to lie in honor in the rotunda of the U.S. Capitol. She was the 31st person, the first woman, and only the second black person to be accorded that honor since the practice began in 1852.

Rosa Parks, age 84, displays a program from the dedication of the Rosa Parks Elementary School in San Francisco, California.

Rosa Parks was always modest about her role in the civil rights movement, giving credit to a higher power for her decision not to give up her seat. "I was fortunate God provided me with the strength I needed at the precise time conditions were ripe for change. I am thankful to him every day that he gave me the strength not to move."

By **Kenneth M. Hare**
The Editorial Page Director at *The Montgomery* (Alabama) *Advertiser*, Hare is also the author of *They Walked to Freedom 1955–1956: The Story of the Montgomery Bus Boycott*.

CIVIL RIGHTS WORKERS:
DEATH IN MISSISSIPPI

The murders of civil rights workers James Chaney, Andrew Goodman, and Michael Schwerner by a conspiracy of police and Ku Klux Klansmen in Mississippi on June 21, 1964, was one of the pivotal events of the civil rights movement. Because two of the victims were white — and their disappearance baffled investigators for almost the entire summer of 1964 — the case became a national preoccupation, bringing the Federal Bureau of Investigation (FBI) and world press attention to tiny Philadelphia, Mississippi, the town where the young men had disappeared.

Mississippi was historically a conservative state where whites exercised considerable control over the majority black population; over the years, it had developed a strong distrustful attitude toward outsiders or anyone who threatened "the southern way of life," meaning segregation and the denial of many basic rights to black people. As early as 1961, civil rights workers had targeted Mississippi for efforts to encourage expanded voting rights, for in its repressive environment, few blacks were allowed to vote. The voter registration work was difficult, however, with volunteers frequently being beaten and arrested.

Fearing that the rest of the United States did not fully understand the importance of these events, the civil rights movement hatched a plan to create the Mississippi Summer Project, later known as Freedom Summer, in which 1,000 northern college students, mostly white, would flood the state to help with voter registration and, by their presence, make Mississippi's situation better known. At the prospect of such an "invasion," local resistance stiffened; belligerent state leaders vowed opposition, and the Ku Klux Klan, a white vigilante group that historically had employed violence and intimidation to enforce regional racial customs, was revived.

On the very first day of Freedom Summer, June 21, the three civil rights workers — Chaney, a local black Mississippian who was 21; Goodman, a 20-year old New York college student; and Schwerner, a social worker from New York's Lower East Side who at 24 was already a veteran activist — drove to the remote black hamlet of Longdale to investigate a recent Klan assault. They had visited previously in the hope of opening a class to teach blacks how to register to vote.

After meeting with their contacts there and viewing the charred remains of a church the Klan had set on fire, the young men were heading west toward the county seat of Philadelphia when Deputy Sheriff Cecil Ray Price stopped them for speeding. He placed them under arrest and escorted them to the Neshoba County jail. The civil rights workers, while naturally suspicious of the local police, did not resist. Like everyone in their movement, they believed in the power of nonviolence and nonconfrontation to attain the goal of racial equality.

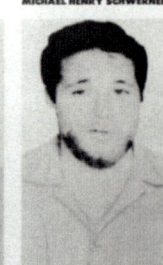

A 44-day FBI search in Mississippi discovered the bodies of the murdered civil rights workers Andrew Goodman, James Early Chaney, and Michael Henry Schwerner.

In 2005, 41 years after the deaths of Goodman, Chaney, and Schwerner, Edgar Ray Killen was convicted of the murders.

They had no way of knowing that Price was part of a Klan conspiracy to hold them in jail until a mob could be assembled.

Later that night the deputy released the three boys, who immediately returned to their car and began driving toward Meridian, where they were based, about a half hour's drive south. Out on the dark rural highway, however, a Klan posse of vehicles, including that of Deputy Price, chased down the civil rights workers. Removing them to a secluded area nearby, the Klansmen pulled their victims from the car, shot and killed them, and secreted their bodies in an earthen dam being built on a neighborhood dairy farm.

A 44-day search ensued, as FBI agents dispatched by President Lyndon Johnson scoured the state. All summer long the world read reports of the mystery, while Mississippi officials refused to even investigate the case, insisting that the disappearance of the men was likely a hoax. When, on August 4, the FBI finally located the dead civil rights workers, a national outcry demanded that those responsible for so heinous a crime be caught and punished.

In the U.S. justice system, murders are normally prosecuted under state law, in the courts of the state where the crime took place. When Mississippi declined to press murder charges, the federal government sought alternatives. Beginning in the 1940s, Washington had tried unsuccessfully to prosecute southern lynch mobs under old Reconstruction-era civil rights laws. It had never done so successfully, but the Justice Department resolved to try again. In early December 1964, the FBI arrested 21 men in the case — local Klansmen and several police officers, among them the Neshoba County sheriff and his deputy — and charged them with conspiracy to violate the three activists' civil rights. Prosecutors were forced to go all the way to the U.S. Supreme Court to have the laws clarified and validated for use in this case. But in 1967, in a landmark verdict, a federal jury of Mississippians found seven of the defendants guilty, and the federal court handed down sentences of up to 10 years.

The murders of Chaney, Goodman, and Schwerner proved a tipping point in overcoming the dogged resistance of "Fortress Mississippi." While some civil rights workers complained that it had taken the deaths of white men finally to bring national scrutiny on Mississippi, the powerful national reaction helped topple the state's particularly vicious forms of racial discrimination once and for all. Today, black Mississippians vote in large numbers, sit in the state legislature, and have represented their state in the U.S. Congress.

In the decades after 1964, many Mississippians grew ashamed of their state's conduct during the civil rights era, and there were calls for the state to come to terms with its mishandling of the affair. On June 21, 2005, exactly 41 years to the day since the three young men had vanished, a Mississippi state court convicted Edgar Ray Killen, a Klan organizer of the conspiracy who had long escaped accountability, of manslaughter. Americans of all races and ethnicities hailed the event as a symbolic victory for justice and a partial resolution of a crime that had long haunted the nation.

By **Philip Dray**
The author of *Capitol Men: The Epic Story of Reconstruction Through the Lives of the First Black Congressmen*, Dray is also the co-author, with Seth Cagin, of *We Are Not Afraid: The Story of Goodman, Schwerner, and Chaney, and the Civil Rights Campaign for Mississippi*.

MEDGAR EVERS:
MARTYR OF THE MISSISSIPPI MOVEMENT

Medgar Evers, head of the National Association for the Advancement of Colored People (NAACP) in Mississippi, was a dynamic leader whose life was cut short by assassination in 1963. His loss at age 37 was a tragic reversal for the civil rights movement, but it galvanized further protest and drew the sympathetic concern of the federal government to his cause.

Born in rural Mississippi in 1925, Evers served with U.S. armed forces in Europe in the Second World War, returning home to attend Alcorn College (a historically black institution located near Lorman, Mississippi), where he was an accomplished student and athlete. There he met his future wife, Myrlie; the couple was married in 1951.

Evers became a protégé of T.R.M. Howard, a black physician and businessman who founded both an insurance agency and a medical clinic in the Mississippi Delta. Howard also established the Mississippi Regional Council of Negro Leadership, a civil rights organization that employed a "top-down" approach, encouraging leading African-American professionals and clergy to promote self-help, business ownership, and, ultimately,

Medgar Evers in 1963. He would be assassinated later that year.

the demand for civil rights among the broader black population.

Evers determined to see the freedoms he had fought for overseas established at home. He soon emerged as one of the Mississippi Regional Council's most effective activists. Like his mentor, he mixed business with civil rights campaigning, working as a salesman for Howard's Magnolia Mutual Life Insurance Company while organizing local chapters of the NAACP and leading boycotts of gas stations that refused blacks access to restrooms. ("Don't Buy Gas Where You Can't Use the Restroom" read one bumper sticker.)

In 1954, Evers challenged the segregationist order by applying for enrollment at the law school of the all-white University of Mississippi, known as "Ole Miss." Evers was turned away, but his effort won him the admiration of the NAACP's Legal Defense Fund, and he was subsequently named the organization's first field secretary in Mississippi, a dangerous and lonely assignment.

"It may sound funny, but I love the South," Evers once said. "I don't choose to live anywhere else. There's land here where a man can raise cattle, and I'm going to do it someday. There are lakes where a man can sink a hook

and fight a bass. There is room here for my children to play and grow and become good citizens — if the white man will let them."

At the time, however, whites' cooperation appeared very much in doubt. Two of the United States' most infamous modern lynchings occurred in Mississippi in those years — the 1955 killing of 14-year-old Emmett Till, and the 1959 lynching of Mack Charles Parker in Poplarville. Evers helped investigate the Till murder, a case that received extensive national attention. Despite strong evidence of the defendants' guilt, an all-white male jury took only 67 minutes to acquit them. One juror later asserted that the panel took a "soda break" to stretch deliberations beyond one hour, "to make it look good." (In May 2004, the Justice Department, calling the 1955 prosecution a "grotesque miscarriage of justice," reopened the murder investigation. But with many potential witnesses long dead and evidence scattered, a grand jury declined to indict the last remaining living suspect.)

Mississippi reacted harshly to the Supreme Court's 1954 *Brown v. Board* of Education ruling and its order to desegregate the nation's public schools. Local white groups known as Citizens Councils vowed to resist integration

Myrlie Evers addresses a Howard University rally after the murder of her husband, Medgar Evers. Myrlie Evers would emerge as a prominent civil rights activist, and later would serve as chairperson of the NAACP.

at any cost. Evers, who had earlier been denied admission to Ole Miss, assisted other blacks' efforts to enroll there. In 1962, Air Force veteran James Meredith was admitted to the school by a direct order from U.S. Supreme Court Justice Hugo Black. State officials resisted the order, and Meredith managed to begin classes only after a night of rioting in which two people were killed and hundreds injured.

As his efforts on Meredith's behalf intensified the segregationist hatred of Evers, he launched a series of boycotts, sit-ins, and protests in Jackson, Mississippi's largest city. Even the NAACP was occasionally concerned with the extent of Evers's efforts. When Martin Luther King Jr. led a high-profile civil rights campaign in Birmingham, Alabama, in the spring of 1963, Evers stepped up his Jackson Movement — demanding the hiring of black police, the creation of a biracial committee, the desegregation of downtown lunch counters, and the use of courtesy titles (Mr., Mrs., Miss) by whites who dealt with black shoppers in downtown stores.

The city's reaction was ominous. Workmen erected on the nearby Mississippi State Fairgrounds a series of fenced stockades capable of holding thousands of protestors — a blunt message to those who considered protesting. Undeterred, Evers and his supporters fought on. Local blacks, including many children, took part in the subsequent rallies and store boycotts, marching and joining picket lines. These demonstrations represented a culmination of Evers's long years of civil rights work. A high point came when Evers appeared on local television to explain the movement's objectives. Whites were not accustomed to seeing black people on TV, especially presenting their case in their own words, and many were outraged.

Soon, attempts were made on Evers's life: A bomb was thrown into his carport, a vehicle nearly ran him over. As Evers returned home on the night of June 12, 1963, he was ambushed and shot as he got out of his car. He died at his own front door.

The murder of so popular a leader enraged the black community. Over several days there were numerous confrontations with police in downtown Jackson. Even the whites who ran the city were shocked by Evers's death, for although he was an agitator, he was at least a familiar presence. The city fathers made the unusual concession of allowing a silent march to honor him, as civil rights leaders from across the nation arrived to pay tribute. He was buried at Arlington National Cemetery in Washington, D.C., with full military honors. Medgar's brother Charles assumed some of his duties with the Jackson campaign, and his widow, Myrlie, became a well-known activist and would serve as chairperson of the NAACP from 1995 to 1998.

It was Medgar Evers's fate to have his name linked with one of the most frustrating legal cases of the civil rights era. His killer, a white supremacist named Byron De La Beckwith, scion of an old Mississippi family, was put on trial twice in the 1960s, but in each instance was acquitted by white juries. Not until 1994, a full three decades after Evers had led his fellow Mississippians in a crusade against bigotry and intolerance, was Beckwith convicted and sentenced to life in prison, where he died in 2001.

Ultimately, Evers triumphed, even in death. The year he was murdered, only 28,000 black Mississippians had successfully registered to vote. By 1971, that number had risen to over a quarter-million and, by 1982, to half a million. By 2006, Mississippi had the highest number of black elected officials in the country, including a quarter of its delegation in the U.S. House of Representatives and some 27 percent of its state legislature.

By **Philip Dray**
The author of *Capitol Men: The Epic Story of Reconstruction Through the Lives of the First Black Congressmen*, Dray is also the co-author, with Seth Cagin, *of We Are Not Afraid: The Story of Goodman, Schwerner, and Chaney, and the Civil Rights Campaign for Mississippi.*

— 6 —
"It Cannot Continue"
ESTABLISHING LEGAL EQUALITY

The civil rights movement led by Martin Luther King Jr. and others was the indispensable catalyst for the passage of two new laws of unparalleled importance. The Civil Rights Act of 1964 and the Voting Rights Act of 1965 at last would establish firmly the legal equality of African Americans. They were enacted partly because of a structural transformation of American politics, including the unexpected elevation of a powerful, pro-civil-rights southern president who helped overcome the forces that had defeated earlier civil rights legislation. Above all, support for these laws came from the growing political constituency for change — the millions of Americans horrified by the actions of segregationists in the South.

Changing Politics

Ever since post-Civil War Reconstruction failed to ensure the civil rights of blacks in the American South, two great obstacles had blocked efforts at the national level to end

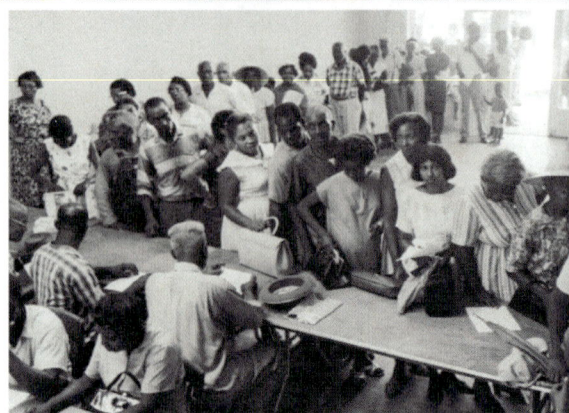

Top to bottom: The Rev. Hosea Williams addresses a 1965 Selma, Alabama voter registration rally.
1966: With the Voting Rights Act now law, Alabama African Americans queue up to register as voters.

Jim Crow: the political party system and the rules of the U.S. Congress. When the United States acquired vast and potentially slaveholding territories (including California and much of today's American Southwest) in the Mexican War of 1846-1848, the nation's political parties increasingly formulated their positions on sectional lines: Democrats favored the South, and the expansion of slavery; Whigs, and later Republicans, favored the North, opposed the extension of slavery into the newly acquired territories, and often believed that complete abolition was only a matter of time. Whigs and Republicans in this era favored the aggressive use of federal power to promote economic development. Southerners and Democrats — fearing federal action against slavery — favored the supremacy of individual states against a federal government properly limited to only those powers specifically granted by the Constitution. This "states' rights" concept has deep roots in American history. Early in the 19th century, however, it became entangled with the issues of slavery, segregation, and civil rights.

These patterns persisted after the Civil War. As we have seen, the post-war Radical Republicans pressed for a Reconstruction that would ensure African-American rights. After Reconstruction, the "Party of Lincoln" — the Republicans — continued to enjoy the support of most blacks. The Democratic Party, meanwhile, evolved into an alliance of southern segregationists and northern urban residents, often immigrants and industrial workers. As the 20th century progressed, the party's northern wing became more politically liberal, and, with President Franklin D. Roosevelt's New Deal economic policies, more accepting of broad federal powers. Liberal northern Democrats often chafed against southern racism, but their party could not compete nationally without the support of the "solid South."

The rules of the U.S. Senate were another formidable obstacle to civil rights legislation. While passing a bill required only a simple majority, any senator could block a vote simply by declining to stop speaking during Senate debate, refusing to relinquish the floor. At that time, a two-thirds majority of senators could vote "cloture" of debate. In practical terms, then, no significant legislation could pass the Senate without the support of two-thirds of its members. This meant that southern senators, elected in states where blacks were routinely deprived of the right to vote, could — and did — block civil rights bills.

Anti-civil-rights filibusters, as these lengthy senatorial speeches came to be known, blocked much legislation over the years. In 1946, a weeks-long filibuster defeated a bill that enjoyed majority support and would have prevented workplace discrimination. In 1957, Senator Strom Thurmond (then a Democratic senator from South Carolina) filibustered for 24 hours and 18 minutes in an unsuccessful effort to block the mild Civil Rights Act of 1957.

But slowly the constellation of political forces was shifting in ways that would prove helpful to the civil rights movement. The black vote, at least in the North, had grown more important. For most of the nation's history, the overwhelming majority of African Americans resided in the South. During the first half of the 20th century, many African Americans began to move from the South to Chicago and other northern cities. An estimated 6 million blacks would head north during this "Great Migration." The North was not free of racial prejudice, but blacks there could vote, and they became an increasingly attractive target for ambitious politicians.

In 1960, the Democratic candidate for president, Senator John F. Kennedy, was determined to increase his share of the historically Republican African-American vote. When Martin Luther King Jr. was jailed following an Atlanta sit-in, Kennedy phoned King's wife, Coretta Scott King, to offer his sympathy, even as his brother, the future attorney general, Robert F. Kennedy, worked to secure King's release. Freed on bail, King acknowledged a "great debt of gratitude to Senator Kennedy and his family." Kennedy carried an estimated 70 percent of the African-American vote in a tight election in which he prevailed over Republican Vice President Richard M. Nixon by less than 1 percent of the popular vote.

While historians differ over the Kennedy administration's civil rights record, it is not unfair to remark that it was better than that of its 20th-century predecessors, but not as strong as civil rights activists would have liked. John and Robert Kennedy repeatedly urged King not to press too hard. But when King would forge ahead, the Kennedys generally would follow.

As previously described, President Kennedy introduced broad civil rights legislation in the aftermath of the events in Birmingham. With Kennedy's assassination in November 1963, responsibility for that legislation would fall to his vice president and successor, Lyndon Johnson.

Lyndon Baines Johnson

The new president possessed two enormous assets: a singularly powerful personality and a mastery of the procedures and personalities of the U.S. Congress perhaps unparalleled in American history. From 1954 to 1960, Johnson had served, in the words of biographer Robert Dallek, as "the most effective majority leader in Senate history." To his command of the Senate's often arcane rules and traditions, Johnson added what one might call intense powers of personal persuasion. "He'd come on just like a tidal wave," said Johnson's vice president, Hubert Humphrey. "He went through walls. ... He'd take the whole room over."

The historian Doris Kearns Goodwin, who served as a White House fellow under Johnson, recalled Johnson's ability to focus all his energies on extracting a needed vote from a recalcitrant senator. She called it "The Treatment." King biographer Marshall Frady described it as

> ... a ferocious manner of persuasion that proceeded by a kind of progressive physical engulfment: wrapping one giant arm around a colleague's shoulder with his other hand clenching his lapel, then straightening the senator's tie knot, then nudging and punching his chest and sticking a forefinger into his shirt. Johnson would lower his face closer and closer to his subject's in escalating exhortation until the man would be bowed backward like a parenthesis mark.

Johnson had been born poor in Texas and understood intimately the conditions under which African Americans and Mexican Americans labored. As a congressman and then senator from a southern state, electoral realities obliged Johnson to mute some of his progressive views on civil rights and racial equality. But elevated unexpectedly to the presidency, Johnson placed the full measure of his political skills to work for the passage of the landmark civil rights laws.

As the new president told Richard Russell, an influential senator from Georgia whose opposition to civil rights legislation posed a formidable obstacle: "I'm not going to cavil and I'm not going to compromise. I'm going to pass it just as it is, Dick, and if you get in my way I'm going to run you down. I just want you to know that because I care about you."

The Civil Rights Act of 1964

For nearly a century, many states had managed to escape the obvious mandate of the Fourteenth Amendment to the U.S. Constitution:

> No State shall make or enforce any law which shall abridge the privileges or immunities of citizens of the United States; nor shall any State deprive any person of life, liberty, or property, without due process of law; nor deny to any person within its jurisdiction the equal protection of the laws.

Court decisions such as *Brown v. Board of Education* and the many others won by Thurgood Marshall and the National Association for the Advancement of Colored People finally established that *government*, even state governments in the Deep South, could not discriminate against African Americans or anyone else. Civil rights activists like the Freedom Riders risked their lives, but at least there was no doubt that the law was on their side and that those who attacked them were lawbreakers.

But the owners of a movie theater or a department store lunch counter were not the government. As a result, the civil rights movement was obliged to wage battles one city and one business at a time. While Rosa Parks's brave refusal to move to the back of the bus led to the desegregation of public transportation in Montgomery, Alabama, hundreds or even thousands more Rosa Parks — and Martin Luther Kings — would be needed to desegregate fully the South.

Plainly, legislation was needed to prohibit acts of private discrimination in public places. Such a law would represent a dramatic expansion of federal authority. The American Constitution explains what the federal — and, in the post-Civil War amendments the state governments — may and may not do. It does not speak of Woolworth's lunch counter.

In the end, proponents of what became the Civil Rights Act of 1964 would assert, and the courts subsequently would accept, that Congress possessed the authority to ban discrimination in employment, public accommodations, and other aspects of life. They pointed to the constitutional provision (Article I, Section 8) authorizing Congress "to regulate Commerce ... among the several States." By the mid-20th century, nearly every economic transaction involved some form of interstate commerce, were one to look closely enough. In 1969, for instance, the Supreme Court, in *Daniel v. Paul*, rejected a discriminatory "entertainment club's" claim that its lack of interstate activity exempted it from the Civil Rights Act. Among the Court's findings: The snack bar served hamburgers and hot dogs on rolls, and the "principal ingredients going into the bread were produced and processed in other States."

President Johnson's introduction of the Civil Rights Act of 1964 provoked one of the nation's great political contests. The act prevailed because much of the nation had looked hard into Bull Connor's eyes and had not liked what it saw. But passage also would require all of Johnson's formidable skills. It was understood that majorities of Republicans and northern Democrats would support the bill, but that Johnson would have to engineer a two-thirds Senate majority to overcome the inevitable filibuster by southern Democrats.

Johnson, in his first State of the Union Address on January 8, 1964, urged Congress to "let this session ... be known as the session which did more for civil rights than the last hundred sessions combined." The months that followed saw intense congressional fact-finding and debate over the act. The House of Representatives held more than 70 days of public hearings, during which some 275 witnesses offered nearly 6,000 pages of testimony. At the end of this process, the House passed the bill by a vote of 290 to 130.

The Senate filibuster would last for 57 days, during which time the Senate conducted virtually no other business. As the speeches continued (one senator carried a 1,500-page speech onto the floor), President Johnson subjected many a senator to "'The Treatment," and a variety of labor, religious, and civil rights groups lobbied for cloture and a final vote. Finally, on June 10, 1964, the Senate voted 71 to 29 to end debate — the first time cloture had ever been successfully invoked in a civil rights matter. A week later, the Senate passed

"It cannot continue … ." President Lyndon B. Johnson signs into law the Civil Rights Act of 1964, in the presence of congressional leaders, and Attorney General Robert F. Kennedy (at rear, directly behind Johnson).

its version of the civil rights bill. On July 2, 1964, the House of Representatives agreed to the Senate version, sending the bill to the White House.

President Johnson affixed his signature that evening, in the course of a nationally televised address. "Americans of every race and color have died in battle to protect our freedom," he told the nation. He continued,

> Americans of every race and color have worked to build a nation of widening opportunities. Now our generation of Americans has been called on to continue the unending search for justice within our own borders.
>
> We believe that all men are created equal. Yet many are denied equal treatment.
>
> We believe that all men have certain unalienable rights. Yet many Americans do not enjoy those rights.
>
> We believe that all men are entitled to the blessings of liberty. Yet millions are being deprived of those blessings — not because of their own failures, but because of the color of their skin.
>
> The reasons are deeply imbedded in history and tradition and the nature of man. We can understand — without rancor or hatred — how this all happened.
>
> But it cannot continue. Our Constitution, the foundation of our Republic, forbids it. ... The purpose of the law is simple.
>
> It does not restrict the freedom of any American, so long as he respects the rights of others.
>
> It does not give special treatment to any citizen.
>
> It does say the only limit to a man's hope for happiness, and for the future of his children, shall be his own ability.
>
> It does say that there are those who are equal before God shall now also be equal in the polling booths, in the classrooms, in the factories ...
>
> My fellow citizens, we have come now to a time of testing. We must not fail.
>
> Let us close the springs of racial poison. Let us pray for wise and understanding hearts. Let us lay aside irrelevant differences and make our nation whole. Let us hasten that day when our unmeasured strength and our unbounded spirit will be free.

FREE AT LAST: THE U.S. CIVIL RIGHTS MOVEMENT 55

Clockwise from above: "We shall overcome." A newly registered voter in Selma, Alabama, August 1965. Civil rights marchers approach Montgomery, Alabama, on the fourth day of the Selma-to-Montgomery march. Americans from across the nation joined in the effort. The four protestors at front hailed from (left to right) New York (first two), Michigan, and Selma, Alabama.
March 1965: A federal marshal reads a court order enjoining a planned voter registration protest march at Selma, Alabama. Dr. King is at right, Andrew Young, a future Ambassador to the United Nations and mayor of Atlanta, Georgia, is at left with arms folded.

The Act's Powers

After two centuries of slavery, segregation, and legal inequality, and the resulting economic disadvantage, the Civil Rights Act of 1964 gave the federal government and private individuals the legal authority they needed to attack squarely racial (and gender — the act also bars discrimination on the basis of sex) discrimination.

This authority is spelled out in broad provisions, called "titles." The major points include:
- Title I, which abolished unequal application of voter registration requirements.
- Title II, which prohibited discrimination in public accommodations. The title authorized individuals to file lawsuits to obtain injunctive relief (a court order ordering someone to do or not to do something) and allowed the attorney general of the United States to intervene in those lawsuits he deemed "of general public importance."
- Title III, which authorized the U.S. attorney general to file a lawsuit, provided the case would "materially further the orderly progress of desegregation in public facilities," where an aggrieved person was unable himself or herself to maintain such a suit.
- Title IV, which authorized the attorney general to file suit to force the desegregation of public schools. This provision aimed to accelerate the slow progress made during the decade since *Brown v. Board of Education*.
- Title VI, which extended the act's provisions to "any program or activity receiving federal financial assistance." It authorized the federal government to withhold federal funds from any such program that practiced discrimination.
- Title VII, which prohibited employment discrimination by any business employing more than 25 people. It established the Equal Employment Opportunity Commission to review complaints of discrimination in recruitment, hiring, compensation, and advancement.

The Voting Rights Act of 1965: The Background

Court decisions and civil rights statutes were crucial tools in establishing, protecting, and enforcing the civil rights of African Americans. The surest way to guarantee the permanence of these rights, however, was to empower blacks politically to assert themselves as full participants in the democratic system. The right to vote, then, was arguably the most fundamental right of all, and one that, practically speaking, African Americans in the South had not enjoyed since the failure of Reconstruction.

Looking back, after the withdrawal of northern armies from the South in 1877, white southern elites re-imposed their political dominance. Suppressing the African-American vote was crucial to this objective and was achieved by a number of methods. At first, raw violence was the preferred tool. A number of other practices developed.

One such practice was the "poll tax." This was a special tax levied equally on every member of a community. Citizens who failed to pay were deemed ineligible to vote. Many southern states introduced poll taxes between 1889 and 1910. Given the extent of African-American poverty, the poll tax disenfranchised large numbers of black voters, and poor whites as well. The Twenty-Fourth Amendment to the U.S. Constitution (1964) prohibited denying any citizen the right to vote in an election for federal office for failure to pay a poll tax. A Supreme Court decision two years later extended this prohibition to state and local elections.

Another practice was the "literacy requirement" for voter registration. Highly subjective oral and written examinations nearly always were applied with special vigor to African-American applicants. Some states would not even permit an applicant to take the examination unless an already-registered voter would vouch for him or her. It was nearly impossible for many black applicants even to take the test, since there were very few African Americans on the southern voting rolls, and few southern whites would risk social ostracism or worse to vouch-in a prospective black voter. The examination was often blatantly unfair. It might require an applicant to write out a passage from the Constitution as dictated by the county registrar — dictated clearly to white applicants, mumbled to blacks.

Southern election officials adopted any number of tactics to prevent black applicants from qualifying. In Alabama, for instance, the decision whether an applicant passed or failed was made in secret, and there was no method for challenging the decisions. Not surprisingly, at least one Alabama board of registrars "qualified" each and every white applicant and not a single black.

Whatever tactic was employed, the threat of violence always lurked in the background. Election officials might publish in local newspapers the names of black voter applicants. This alerted local white Citizens Councils and Ku Klux Klan chapters to blacks who might need to be "persuaded" to withdraw their applications.

Against this background of violent intimidation, activists from the Student Nonviolent Coordinating Committee and the Congress of Racial Equality, among others, launched voter registration campaigns in rural and heavily black parts of the Deep South in 1961. The work took incredible courage. As an early volunteer, the plantation worker Fannie Lou Hamer, memorably explained: "I guess if I'd had any sense, I'd have been scared — but what was the point of being scared? The only thing they [white people] could do was kill me, and it seemed they'd been trying to do that a little at a time since I could remember."

In 1964, the Southern Christian Leadership Conference, the Congress of Racial Equality, the National Association for the Advancement of Colored People, and the Student Nonviolent Coordinating Committee launched the "Freedom Summer." More than 1,000 northern whites, mostly college students, volunteered to travel to Mississippi and help black voters register. Their presence also was intended to draw national attention to the violent suppression of black voting rights.

On June 21, the very first day of Freedom Summer, the volunteers achieved this goal in a tragic manner. Three civil rights workers, African American James Chaney and two white Jewish Americans, Michael Schwerner and Andrew Goodman, were reported missing and later found murdered. Their murder forced Americans to confront more directly the related issues of voting rights and violence. While the brave volunteers persuaded some 17,000 equally brave African Americans to complete voter registration applications, election officials ultimately accepted less than 10 percent of these. Blacks, more and more Americans understood, comprised nearly half of Mississippi's population but only 5 percent of its registered voters.

Bloody Sunday in Selma

The following year, civil rights organizations launched a registration drive in Selma, Alabama, a small city about 50 miles west of Montgomery. There were about 15,000 blacks residing in Selma, but only 350 had successfully registered to vote. At a February 1965 voting rights rally in nearby Marion, police shot and killed a young black man named Jimmie Lee Jackson.

In response, activists called a March 7 march from Selma to the Alabama state capitol at Montgomery. Led by John Lewis of SNCC and Martin Luther King's aide, the Reverend Hosea Williams, some 525 marchers were met on the Pettus Bridge over the Alabama River by Alabama state troopers and local lawmen. They had gas masks at hand and nightsticks at the ready. The trooper leader (Major John Cloud) ordered the marchers to return to their church. Reverend Williams answered: "May we have a word with the major?" "There is no word to be had," came the reply.

The suppression of the march, the *New York Times* reported, "was swift and thorough." The paper described a flying wedge of troopers and recounted how "the first 10 or 20 Negroes were swept to the ground screaming, arms and

"Bloody Sunday," Selma, Alabama, March 7, 1965. The suppression of the first Selma-to-Montgomery civil rights march was swift and thorough. "I thought I saw death," said future U.S. Representative John Lewis.

legs flying." With the news media on hand and recording their actions for a horrified national audience, the troopers fired tear gas canisters. Local law enforcement pursued the retreating protestors with whips and nightsticks. "I was hit in the head by a state trooper with a nightstick ... I thought I saw death," said Lewis, hospitalized with a concussion.

For millions of Americans, March 7, 1965, would be known simply as Bloody Sunday. Typical was the reaction of U.S. Representative James G. O'Hara of Michigan, who called the day's events "a savage action, storm-trooper style, under direction of a reckless demagogue [a reference to Alabama's governor, George Wallace]."

From Atlanta, Martin Luther King Jr. announced that he and Ralph Abernathy would lead a second Selma-to-Montgomery march that Tuesday. He called on "religious leaders from all over the nation to join us on Tuesday in our peaceful, nonviolent march for freedom." Before the march could occur, a federal judge, not unfriendly to the activists but determined to hold hearings before acting, issued a court order temporarily forbidding the march.

King was under intense political pressure from every corner. Federal officials urged him to delay the march. With the judge's injunction now in place, King and his followers would be the lawbreakers should the march proceed. But

Marchers cross the Edmund Pettis bridge over the Alabama River, March 21, 1965, the beginning of the third Selma-to-Montgomery march.

younger activists, many affiliated with SNCC, wanted to move faster. King risked losing his place at the head of the movement were he unable to satisfy their demands.

On March 9, King and Abernathy led some 3,000 peaceful protestors — their black followers joined by hundreds of white religious leaders — on the second Selma-to-Montgomery march. Troopers again met them at the Pettus Bridge. The marchers stopped, then sang the movement's anthem: "We Shall Overcome." The group then prayed, and Abernathy thanked God for the marchers who "came to present their bodies as a living sacrifice." King then directed his followers to turn back. "As a nonviolent, I couldn't move people into a potentially violent situation," he told the *Washington Post*.

King's decision disappointed some of the more zealous activists. But King had been conferring quietly with federal officials. The events of Bloody Sunday also had exerted great pressure on an already sympathetic President Johnson. Too many Americans at long last had seen enough. From religious groups and state legislatures, youthful protestors and members of Congress, the demand for federal action was growing. The two leaders appear to have struck a tacit bargain: King would not violate the injunction, and the Johnson administration quietly suggested it would soon be lifted.

On March 15, Johnson introduced the legislation that would become the Voting Rights Act. Addressing the nation that night, President Johnson employed the plainest of language in the service of a basic American value — the right to vote:

There is no Negro problem. There is no southern problem. There is no northern problem. There is only an American problem.

And we are met here tonight as Americans ... to solve that problem.

The Constitution says that no person shall be kept from voting because of his race or his color. We have all sworn an oath before God to support and to defend that Constitution.

We must now act in obedience to that oath. ...

There is no constitutional issue here. The command of the Constitution is plain. There is no moral issue. It is wrong — deadly wrong — to deny any of your fellow Americans the right to vote in this country. There is no issue of States rights or National rights. There is only the struggle for human rights. ...

What happened in Selma is part of a far larger movement which reaches into every section and State of America. It is the effort of American Negroes to secure for themselves the full blessings of American life.

"We have come from three centuries of suffering and hardship." The marchers arrive at Montgomery.

Their cause must be our cause too, because it is not just Negroes but really it is all of us who must overcome the crippling legacy of bigotry and injustice. And we shall overcome.

Two days later, the federal court lifted the injunction against the marchers. U.S. District Judge Frank M. Johnson Jr. further ordered that state and county authorities not interfere and indeed take affirmative measures to protect the activists. "The law is clear," the judge wrote, "that the right to petition one's government for the redress of grievances may be exercised in large groups ... and these rights may be exercised by marching, even along public highways."

The Selma-to-Montgomery March

By March 21, thousands of Americans from all walks of life began to assemble in Selma for the third Selma-to-Montgomery march. The marchers planned to cover the entire 87-kilometer route over the course of five days and four nights, with marchers sleeping under the stars. The route they followed is today a National Historic Trail.

With the support of the Johnson administration and an aroused American people, the difference from the earlier efforts could not be more apparent. Major John Cloud of the Alabama State Troopers had ordered the beatings and gassings two weeks earlier. Now he was obliged to occupy the lead car accompanying the protestors across the Pettus Bridge. Federal military police were on hand to provide protection, and elements of the Alabama National Guard were temporarily placed under federal command. As more than 3,000 marchers began the first leg of their quest, Abernathy told them, "When we get to Montgomery, we are going to go up to Governor Wallace's door and say, 'George, it's all over now. We've got the ballot.'"

"Walk together, children," King instructed, "and don't you get weary, and it will lead us to a Promised Land."

The *New York Times* offered this description of the crowd as it set out along U.S. Highway 80:

> There were civil rights leaders and rabbis, pretty coeds and bearded representatives of the student left, movie stars and infants in strollers. There were two blind people and a man with one leg. But mostly there were the Negroes who believe they have been denied the vote too long.

The marchers covered a bit over 11 kilometers that first day, then pitched two large circus tents and slept in sleeping bags and blankets. The next morning King announced: "I am happy to say that I have slept in a sleeping bag for the first time in my life. I feel fine." By the second day, though, blisters and sunburn were common.

Because the highway narrowed in rural areas, the federal court had ruled that only 300 marchers could participate until the road widened again outside Montgomery. But a fair number of "extras" chose to tag along, even during the third day, which was marked by torrential rains. The marchers responded in song; among their selections: "Ain't Gonna Let Nobody Turn Me 'Round" and "We Shall Overcome."

King briefly left the march to deliver a long-scheduled address in Cleveland, Ohio. There King made explicit his debt to Mahatma Gandhi, whose famous march to the sea anticipated the Selma-to-Montgomery trek. "We are challenged to make the world one in terms of brotherhood," King said. "We must learn to live together as brothers, or we will all perish as fools."

As the marchers approached Montgomery, the crowd swelled to 25,000 or more. They came by chartered plane, by bus, and by rail. A delegation of leading American historians arrived to participate in the final leg. They issued a statement: "We believe it is high time for the issues over which the Civil War was fought to be finally resolved." The singer and civil rights activist Harry Belafonte enlisted an all-star group of Hollywood entertainers.

On March 25, with Martin Luther King at the head, the activists entered Montgomery. They marched up Dexter Avenue, tracing the path traversed a century ago by the inaugural parade of Jefferson Davis, first and only president of the Confederate States of America, the would-be nation whose championing of slavery sparked the Civil War. Now, a century later, the descendants of black slaves approached the state house to demand the rights to which they had long been entitled, and long been denied. Their petition read:

> We have come not only five days and 50 miles [80 kilometers], but we have come from three centuries of suffering and hardship. We have come to you, the Governor of Alabama, to declare that we must have our freedom NOW. We must have the right to vote; we must have equal protection of the law, and an end to police brutality.

Governor Wallace had already fled the scene. It didn't matter.

King delivered that day one of his most famous speeches, one in which he quoted a 70-year-old participant in the Montgomery bus boycott. Asked one day whether she would not have preferred riding to walking, Mother Pollard replied: "My feets is tired, but my soul is rested."

"How long? Not long. Because no lie can live forever," said Martin Luther King, Jr. at the end of the Selma-to-Montgomery march. Pictured here: King delivering a sermon at his Ebenezer Baptist Church in Atlanta, Georgia.

The just concluded march, King said, was "a shining moment in the conscience of man." He singled out as honorable and inspiring "the pilgrimage of clergymen and laymen of every race and faith pouring into Selma to face danger at the side of its embattled Negroes." "Like an idea whose time has come," King continued, "not even the marching of mighty armies can halt us. We are moving to the land of freedom."

> We must come to see that the end we seek is a society at peace with itself, a society that can live with its conscience. That will be a day not of the white man, not of the black man. That will be the day of man as man.
>
> I know you are asking today, "How long will it take?" I come to say to you this afternoon however difficult the moment, however frustrating the hour, it will not be long, because truth pressed to earth will rise again.
>
> How long? Not long, because no lie can live forever.
>
> How long? Not long, because you still reap what you sow.
>
> How long? Not long. Because the arm of the moral universe is long but it bends toward justice.

The Voting Rights Act Enacted

Five months later, the Congress passed and President Johnson signed into law the Voting Rights Act of 1965. Shortly before noon on August 6, 1965, Johnson drove to the U.S. Capitol building. Waiting for him were the leaders of Congress and of the civil rights movement, Martin Luther King Jr. and John Lewis among them. In signing the act into law, Johnson told the nation:

> The central fact of American civilization ... is that freedom and justice and the dignity of man are not just words to us. We believe in them. Under all the growth, and the tumult, and abundance, we believe. And so, as long as some among us are oppressed and we are part of that oppression, it must blunt our faith and sap the strength of our high purpose.
>
> Thus this is a victory for the freedom of the American Negro, but it is also a victory for the freedom of the American nation. And every family across this great entire searching land will live stronger in liberty, will live more splendid in expectation, and will be prouder to be American because of the act that you have passed that I will sign today.

What the Act Does

The Fifteenth Amendment already barred racial discrimination in voting rights, so the problem was not that African Americans lacked the legal right to vote. It was that some state and local officials had systematically deprived blacks of those rights. The Voting Rights Act accordingly authorized the federal government to assume control of the voter registration process in any state or voting district that had in 1964 employed a literacy or other qualifying test and in which fewer than half of voting age residents had either registered or voted. Six entire southern states were thus "covered," as were a number of counties in several other states. Covered jurisdictions were prohibited from modifying their voting rules and regulations without first affording federal officials the opportunity to review the change for discriminatory intent or effect. Other provisions barred the future use of literacy tests and directed the attorney general of the United States to commence legal action to end the use of poll taxes in state elections. (The Twenty-Fourth Amendment to the U.S. Constitution, ratified in January 1964, already barred the poll tax in elections for federal office.)

The introduction of federal "examiners" ended the mass intimidation of potential minority voters. The results were dramatic. By the end of 1965, the five states of the Deep South alone registered 160,000 new African-American voters. By 2000, African-American registration rates trailed that of whites by only 2 percent. In the South, where in 1965 only two African Americans served either in the U.S. Congress or a state legislature, the number today is 160.

The Voting Rights Act was originally enacted for a five-year period, but it has been both extended and expanded to introduce new requirements, such as the provision of bilingual election materials.

In 1982, President Ronald Reagan signed a 25-year extension: "The right to vote is the crown jewel of American liberties," he said, "and we will not see its luster diminished." President George W. Bush signed another 25-year extension in 2006.

WHITE SOUTHERNERS' REACTIONS TO THE CIVIL RIGHTS MOVEMENT

African Americans who waged epic struggles for civil rights also altered white Southerners' worlds. Some whites embraced the prospect of a new interracial land. Many more reacted with hostility. They feared social and political change, and grappled uncomfortably with the fact that their way of life seemed gone for good.

The "Southern way of life" encompassed a distinctive mix of economic, social, and cultural practices — symbolized by the fragrant magnolia, the slow pace of life, and the sweet mint julep, a popular alcoholic beverage. It also contained implications about the region's racial order — one in which whites wielded power and blacks accommodated. Centuries of slavery and decades of segregation cemented a legal and political system characterized by white dominance. By the 20th century, "Jim Crow" had become a shorthand for legalized segregation. (That phrase derived from the name of a character in a 19th century minstrel show in which whites wore blackface makeup and caricatured slave culture.) Massive inequalities marked every facet of daily life. Blacks always addressed whites as "Mr." or "Mrs.," though whites seldom bestowed such courtesy titles on African Americans. Blacks labored in white homes as nannies, cooks, maids, and yardmen. Whites expected docility; black resistance seemed unfathomable.

Through the long years of slavery and segregation, white Southerners produced and absorbed cruel stereotypes about African Americans: that they were unclean and shiftless, unintelligent and oversexed. Blacks became either clowns or savages, with no area in between. Whites often defined themselves — their status, identities, daily lives, and self-worth — in relation to these concocted notions about African Americans. If blacks were submissive and infantile, whites were strong and dignified. Blackness meant degradation; to be free was to be white. The civil rights struggle threatened to hoist African Americans up and out of this social "place" that whites had created for them. White Southerners would find blacks in their schools and neighborhoods, their restaurants, and polling places. Many whites feared this vision of the Southern future.

Many white Southerners came to believe that African Americans abided — and even enjoyed — their roles as second-class citizens. When the civil rights movement tore through the South in the 1950s and 1960s, it exposed the falsity of such beliefs. At long last, African Americans voiced their discontent and demanded dignity. Black rebellion clashed so sharply with white perceptions that many disbelieved their own eyes. And as grassroots organizers led a mass movement for black equality, whites rose up in resistance.

The U.S. Supreme Court, with its 1954 decision in *Brown v. Board of Education*, ensured that Southern schools would become the first battlegrounds. The court ruled that segregated schools stamped black children with a "badge of inferiority," and that Southern states must integrate their schools "with all deliberate speed."

Demonstrators protesting the integration of a New Orleans, Louisiana, public elementary school, 1960.

Southern politicians denounced the court ruling. In language that played upon whites' underlying racial fears and stoked contempt for the federal government, senators such as Harry Byrd of Virginia claimed the court had overstepped its bounds. White Southerners tried to circumvent the order, and rallied to beat back desegregation at every turn. Local leaders and businessmen organized themselves into Citizens Councils, groups that visited economic reprisal upon any blacks — or whites — who dared advocate integration.

In 1957, a federal court ordered integration of the Little Rock, Arkansas, public schools. Nine blacks were selected to enroll in Little Rock's Central High School, but Governor Orval Faubus blocked the students from the schoolhouse door. After initial reluctance, President Dwight Eisenhower mobilized a battle group of the U.S. Army's 101st Airborne Division to enforce the court order by escorting the "Little Rock Nine" to class. When several African-American teenagers finally arrived at Central, they encountered a vicious white mob. Parents jeered the incoming students and the federal marshals who protected them. Enraged white Southerners deplored a scene they thought had died with Reconstruction: that of federal troops protecting blacks' civil rights in the South.

A similar conflagration erupted in New Orleans when that city became the first in the Deep South to desegregate. In November 1960, four African-American girls integrated Frantz Elementary School in the city's Ninth Ward. That neighborhood was one of the city's poorest. In addition to grievances against organized blacks and an active federal government, white Southerners also felt deep class divides. White Ninth Ward residents believed that the city's rich and powerful had foisted integration upon them — and them alone. Across the region, poor whites shouldered the "burden" of integration. If the upper classes maintained social safety valves like country clubs, private schools, and exclusive suburbs, poorer whites confronted the fact that their public schools, swimming pools, and neighborhoods were often the first to experience desegregation.

Millions of white Southerners found champions in politicians such as Alabama's governor, George Wallace, who both cultivated and exploited for political gain a deep anti-civil-rights sentiment. In his 1963 inaugural address, Wallace declared: "Segregation now, segregation tomorrow, segregation forever." He became the very picture of white resistance. Members of the Ku Klux Klan — a violent organization driven by racism, anti-Semitism, and nativism — persisted in a similar delusion: that the bloodshed they inflicted could postpone the day of racial equality. In 1963 in Birmingham, Alabama, Klansmen bombed a black Baptist church and killed four girls. The next year, Klansmen in Philadelphia, Mississippi, murdered three civil rights workers and buried them under an earthen dam. Such gruesome violence sickened many white Southerners, and rifts emerged within the white South. Still, a majority desired the same end — a return to the nostalgic days when blacks doffed their hats to whites and acquiesced to their roles in the segregated Jim Crow order.

Extremism on one side often handed victory to the other. The Klan's horrifying violence pricked white America's conscience and, ultimately, moved the nation closer to passage of epic civil rights legislation — the 1964 Civil Rights Act and the 1965 Voting Rights Act. When President Lyndon Johnson, himself a native Texan and a Southerner, helped usher the legislation through Congress, white Southerners felt betrayed.

The Civil Rights Act integrated businesses and public facilities. Suddenly, whites had to serve blacks in their stores and dine beside them at restaurants. Such changes shattered the rhythm of white southerners' daily lives. Many whites denounced the "Civil Wrongs Bill," holding that such federal laws imperiled their own rights. They clung to the notion that rights were finite, and that as blacks gained freedom, whites must suffer a loss of their own liberties. On the precarious seesaw of Southern race relations, whites thought they would plummet if blacks ascended.

Often hooded, members of the Ku Klux Klan advocated white supremacy and employed terrorism, violence, and lynching against African Americans, Jews, and Roman Catholics, among others.

Throughout black-majority areas, the Voting Rights Act granted African Americans a stunning new power. In these citadels of the old slave South, where whites were outnumbered by a ratio of almost four-to-one, blacks voted some of their own into political office. In several rural locales, like Macon County and Greene County, Alabama, African Americans suddenly wielded political power. Before the civil rights years, few whites could have conceived of such transformations. By the 1970s, the previously unthinkable became political reality.

The civil rights movement forever altered white Southerners' everyday lives, upended their traditional attitudes about blacks, and, in some towns, shifted the balance of political power. It stripped the veneers of docility from African Americans and invested them with a new dignity. Life seemed unrecognizable to many white Southerners. Confronted with a reality they had barely contemplated, some whites retaliated with any weapons at their disposal. Others attempted to avoid the upheaval; they tried to maintain cherished ways of life even as the ground shifted beneath their feet. In the end, evasion proved impossible.

While whites fought the civil rights movement with varying strategies of resistance, few escaped its long reach.

In the end, the civil rights movement transformed the South and the nation. As it changed Southerners' lives and minds, some whites felt they had been liberated — freed from the mandate to degrade and oppress, free from the roles they assumed in the constricting racial hierarchy. Into the 21st century, however, racial inequality continues to haunt American life. Black Americans remain disproportionately impoverished, imprisoned, and undereducated. Yet many ghosts of the Jim Crow South have vanished. After the civil rights movement, African Americans could attend integrated schools, they ran for — and won — political office, and they lived with a dignity that the culture of Jim Crow had denied. These changes also seeped into white Southern life and reshaped its very contours. The civil rights movement pushed Southerners, black and white alike, further along the path toward racial equality.

By **Jason Sokol**
A Mellon Postdoctoral Fellow at the University of Pennsylvania, Sokol is also the author of *There Goes My Everything: White Southerners in the Age of Civil Rights*.

Lunchtime in an integrated public school.

EPILOGUE

More than any time in our nation's history, we are all Americans.

On March 21, 1965, as civil rights advocates and their supporters gathered in Selma, a local Southern Christian Leadership Conference leader warned the press that the "irresponsibility" of the more militant activists might cause the movement enormous harm. The Reverend Jefferson P. Rogers was referring to the Student Nonviolent Coordinating Committee, whose leadership was growing increasingly impatient with the gradualist strategy of Martin Luther King and the mainstream civil rights movement. Nearly every broad-based social movement faces similar tensions, but the years and decades that followed would prove the wisdom of the strategy pursued by Thurgood Marshall, King, and the others. The great triumphs of the civil rights movement were evidence that, in a nation of laws, the key to progress lay in establishing the real legal equality of African Americans — in public facilities, in places of education, and, most of all, at the voting booth.

But this truth was not yet apparent. By May 1966, Stokley Carmichael, veteran of numerous voter registration drives, had established himself as the new head of SNCC. In a speech at Greenwood, Mississippi, Carmichael raised a call for "Black Power." Where Thurgood Marshall and Martin Luther King Jr. had sought integration, Carmichael instead sought separation. Integration, he said, was "an insidious subterfuge, for the maintenance of white supremacy." Meanwhile, the Black Panther Party, (some accounts trace the name to a visual emblem for illiterate voters used in an Alabama voter registration drive) founded in Oakland, California, in October 1966 by activists Huey P. Newton and Bobby Seale, employed armed members — "Panthers" — to shadow police officers whom they believed unfairly targeted blacks. While the party briefly enjoyed a measure of popularity, particularly through its social services programs, armed altercations with local police resulted in the death or jailing of prominent Panthers, turned many Americans against its violent ways, and fragmented the Panther movement. It petered out in a maze of factionalism and mutual recriminations.

The year 1968 was one of political upheaval throughout much of the Western world. In the United States, that year would see the assassination of Senator Robert F. Kennedy, who as attorney general had provided timely assistance to civil rights activists. And it would see the end of King's remarkable career.

It was a measure of the civil rights movement's accomplishments in securing legal equality that King dedicated his last years to fighting for economic equality. On April 3, 1968, he campaigned in Memphis, Tennessee, on behalf of striking — and primarily black — sanitation workers. King's last address drew strongly on his lifelong study of the Bible. It would prove prophetic:

> Well, I don't know what will happen now; we've got some difficult days ahead. But it really doesn't matter with me now, because I've been to the mountaintop. And I don't mind. Like anybody, I would like to live a long life — longevity has its place. But I'm not concerned about that now. I just want to do God's will. And He's allowed me to go up to the mountain. And I've looked over, and I've seen the Promised Land. I may not get there with you. But I want you to know tonight that we, as a people, will get to the Promised Land. And so I'm happy tonight; I'm not worried about anything; I'm not fearing any man. Mine eyes have seen the glory of the coming of the Lord.

An assassin's bullet took King's life the very next day. He was 39 years old. The medical examiners said he died with the heart of a 60 year old, because King had for so long carried the burden of so many. Some 300,000 Americans attended his funeral.

The murder of Martin Luther King Jr. set off riots in Washington, D.C., and in more than 100 other American cities. At that moment, the short of vision and the faint of heart might have questioned King's life work. But the Promised Land that King described was in many ways far closer than it seemed on those angry, fire-lit nights of April 1968.

Owning a home long has been a large part of the American Dream. Left: Forty-two years after her friend Denise McNair was murdered by racist vigilantes, Condoleezza Rice took office as the nation's Secretary of State.

The Triumphs of the Civil Rights Movement

The historical experience of African Americans will always be unique. But meaningful federal enforcement of the right to vote equipped black Americans with the tools that immigrants and other minority groups long have used to pursue — and achieve — the American Dream. In the United States, people who vote wield real political power. With the vote — and the passage of time — legal and political equality for African Americans has produced gains in nearly every walk of life.

John R. Lewis, for example, was one of the Freedom Riders beaten bloody by the Montgomery mob in 1961. Today he represents Georgia's Fifth District in the U.S. House of Representatives. Nearly 50 of his colleagues are African Americans, and several of them wield great political power as chairpersons of influential congressional committees.

President-elect Barack Obama addresses a Chicago crowd on the night of his election to the presidency.

In 1963, Denise McNair was among the girls killed when racist vigilantes bombed Birmingham's Sixteenth Street Baptist Church. In 2005, her friend Condoleezza Rice took office as the nation's secretary of state.

Black secondary school graduation rates have nearly tripled since 1966, and the rate of poverty has been nearly halved in that time. The emergence of a black middle class is a widely noted social development, as are the many successful African-American entrepreneurs, scholars, and literary and artistic achievers.

Although Americans continue to wrestle with racial issues, those issues differ profoundly from those addressed by Thurgood Marshall, Martin Luther King, and the civil rights movement. While today's questions are no less real, they also reflect the genuine progress achieved over the decades that followed.

Consider education, the subject of the *Brown v. Board of Education* decision. Recent Supreme Court decisions explore the permissible limits of "affirmative action" policies that seek to redress past discrimination and to require or encourage that public institutions reflect demographically the communities they serve.

Judges are now asked to decide the competing needs in, for example, a school district that allows all parents to select their children's school. If too many request a particular school, only some students may attend their first-choice institution. In that case, may the district assert, even as a "tiebreaker," its desire to maintain a racial balance in that popular school to determine which requests will be honored?

Should government intervene when schools are effectively segregated because of new housing patterns, and not, as in Linda Brown's day, because millions of African-American students were purposely segregated and relegated to shabby, inferior schools?

Americans of all stripes can and do disagree over issues like this. And few American leaders have answers to these dilemmas.

As this book goes to press, Barack Obama, the son of a black man from Kenya and a white woman from Kansas, has been elected President of the United States. In a campaign speech on race in America, Obama said that

the answer to the slavery question was already embedded within our Constitution — a Constitution that had at its very core the ideal of equal citizenship under the law; a Constitution that promised its people liberty, and justice, and a union that could be and should be perfected over time.

And, as the President-elect told the nation on the night of his electoral triumph

If there is anyone out there who still doubts that America is a place where all things are possible; who still wonders if the dream of our founders is alive in our time; who still questions the power of our democracy, tonight is your answer.

Obama's victory is one measure of the nation's progress. Another measure, surely the most important of all, is the emergence, not least among the younger Americans who will build the nation's future, of a broad and deep consensus that the shameful histories of slavery, segregation, and disadvantage must be relegated to the past.

Executive Editor: **George Clack**
Editor-in-Chief: **Mildred Solà Neely**
Managing Editor: **Michael Jay Friedman**
Art Director: **Min-Chih Yao**
Photo Research: **Maggie Johnson Sliker**

Michael Jay Friedman, the author of this volume's principal text, is Division Chief for Print Publications at the Department of State's Bureau of International Information Programs. He holds a PhD in U.S. political and diplomatic history.

U.S. DEPARTMENT OF STATE
Bureau of International Information Programs
2008
http://www.america.gov

Photo credits:

Picture credits for illustrations appearing top to bottom are separated by dashes and from left to right by semicolons.

Cover: AP Images (4). Inside Front Cover: AP Images. Page 3: Schomburg Center/Art Resource, NY. 4: British Library/London/Great Britain/HIP/Art Resource, NY. 6: Hulton Archive/Getty Images. 8: The Bridgeman Art Library/Getty Images. 9: Library of Congress. 10: Hulton Archive/Getty Images. 11: Painting by Jerry Pinkney, National Geographic Society. 12: MPI/Getty Images. 13: Hulton Archive/Getty Images — Library of Congress, Prints and Photographs Division. 14: Library of Congress, Prints and Photographs Division. 16: Library of Congress, Prints and Photographs Division. 17: Louie Psihoyos/Science Faction. 18: Library of Congress, Prints and Photographs Division. 19: © CORBIS. 20: Library of Congress, Prints and Photographs Division. 21: AP Images. 22: Marie Hansen/Time Life Pictures/Getty Images. 24: Library of Congress, Prints and Photographs Division. 25: © David J. & Janice L. Frent Collection/CORBIS. 26: Scurlock Studio Records, Archives Center, National Museum of American History, Behring Center, Smithsonian Institution. 27: Library of Congress, Prints and Photographs Division; AP Images. 28: Virginia Historical Society, with permission from Afro-American Newspaper Archives and Research Center. 29: © Bettmann/CORBIS — © Jack Moebes/CORBIS; AP Images. 31: AP Images. 33: © Bettmann/CORBIS — AP Images. 35: Don Cravens/Time Life Pictures/Getty Images — Montgomery County Sheriff's Office/AP Images. 36: © Bettmann/CORBIS. 37: Sy Kattelson, Gelatin silver print, 1948, National Portrait Gallery, Smithsonian Institution. 38: © Bettmann/CORBIS (2). 39: Paul Schutzer/Time Life Pictures/Getty Images. 40: Horace W. Cort/AP Images; © Bettmann/CORBIS. 43: Bill Hudson/AP Images. 44: Harry Harry/AP Images.Hulton Archives/CNP/Getty Images. 46: Carlos Osorio/AP Images — Gene Herrick/AP Images. 47: Lacy Adkins/AP Images. 48: © Bettmann/CORBIS. 49: Landall Kyle Carter/CORBIS. 50: AP Images. 51: © Bettmann/CORBIS. 52: © Flip Schulke/CORBIS (2). 55: AP Images. 56: AP Images; Dozier Mobley/AP Images — AP Images. 58,59: AP Images (3). 60: © Flip Schulke/CORBIS. 62-63: © Bettmann/CORBIS; Hoarce W. Cort/AP Images. 64: Bill Eppridge/Time Life Pictures/Getty Images. 65: Digital Vision/Getty Images. 66: Ariel Skelley/Getty Images — Bebeto Matthews/AP images.

Made in the USA
Middletown, DE
15 August 2019